INSPIRING PARENTHOOD

BY DR. JANICE PRESSER

Some couples are like hard-boiled eggs. They're firm and well done, but they can't get very close to each other. They may shatter each other's shell, but even that just brings their outer beings (the white part) together. Their inner selves (the yolks) are isolated from each other. The hard-boiled-egg couples have what's termed a "marriage of convenience." No risk; little intimacy.

Other couples are like soft-boiled eggs. One healthy confrontation and they're a messy puddle, impossible to put back together for a bit more cooking. Very young couples, especially those who have been forced to marry because of untimely pregnancies, are often soft-boiled egg couples. High-risk; intimacy only when the inner selves are shattered.

Then there are the scrambled eggs. They have even given up their uniqueness to create a single, homogenized entity. They may have a feeling of "us against the world," but it is a false feeling of security, since neither can function well alone. If there are children, they, too, may be expected to become part of the omelet, submerging themselves in the family. Low-risk for the couple; high risk for their children; and a largely false sense of intimacy.

Successful couples are like fried eggs, sunny-side up. When they are cracked open against the side of the pan, they obligingly plop in, their outer selves attracted to each other, coming together to form a mutual environment for the two yolks. The yolks may move around in their white field, sometimes touching and sometimes moving apart, yet they always retain their individuality. They risk moving against each other with enough force to break one or both, but their mutual base tends to slow down any confrontation. Their intimacy has room for additional little eggs; children are no major threat, since there is space for them to develop as individuals too. Acceptable risk; high probability of intimacy; and personal growth is enabled for all.

Copyright © 1986 by Dr. Janice Presser
ISBN: 978-1-951510-99-2
All rights reserved. No part of this book may be used or reproduced in any manner
whatsoever without written permission except in the case of
brief quotations embodied in critical articles and reviews
For information address Crossroad Press at 141 Brayden Dr., Hertford, NC 27944
A Panta Rei Production - Panta Rei is an imprint of Crossroad Press.
www.crossroadpress.com

Crossroad Press Trade Edition

Acknowledgments

This book was originally published in the United States of America by Ballantine Books, a division of Random House, Inc., New York, and simultaneously in Canada by Random House of Canada Limited, Toronto, September 1986. The second edition was published in mass market paperback, June 1990. This is the third edition, updated for 2019 and beyond, though much is the same.

The first two editions were dedicated to my parents, Murray and Esther Presser, for surviving my childhood and being the very best grandparents Marni and Andrew could ever have. Although they are no longer alive on earth, they are very much alive in our hearts.

This edition acknowledges that years may pass, but parenting is a lifelong endeavor. And, though I am still the mom, Andrew and Marni continue to remind me that parenting—like most other things worth doing—is a team sport.

The original manuscript also acknowledged the editors for their support thus: A special note of thanks to Michelle Rapkin and Toinette Lippe, who had enduring faith in this book and my ability to write it even when I nearly lost mine.

Preface to the First Edition

Inspiring Parenthood is parenting with grace.

Inspiring Parenthood is recognizing the coming of a child, the becoming of two parents, as a divine gift.

"A baby," wrote Carl Sandburg, "is God's opinion that the world should go on." And, indeed, for most expectant and new parents, a baby is God's opinion that they and their family should go on.

But for some parents this inherent grace, this testimony to joy and promise, is lost in the day-to-day trials and tribulations of life with a baby. Almost overcome by piles of unwashed laundry, overstretched budgets, and quickly regretted words of frustration, the dignity, courage, and reverence of parenting can be submerged by the fear and pain that are the hallmarks of loss of inspiration.

A recent, albeit unscientific, survey by columnist Ann Landers confirmed the depressing view of parenthood as an obstacle to a satisfying life: the majority of her respondents said that if they had their lives to live over again, they would not choose to have children. If parenthood is a state of grace, why do so many parents feel they have lost their inspiration? The twin objectives of this book are to answer that question and to propose a way for parents to avoid the pitfalls that contribute to this joyless state. Please note that although the chapters follow the chronology of parenting, several focus on a theme that is present throughout the life cycle.

If you are expecting a baby or are just beginning to think about marriage and family, it is my hope that this book will help you develop your natural ability to be an inspiring parent.

If your children are already born and you feel that you have lost your inspiration, I hope it will help you find a way to regain the joy that you and your family were meant to have.

J. P.
June 17, 1985

NOTE TO THE READER

I'm leaving the gist of the original note here, even though if I were writing it today, I would try to write gender-free. It's not a binary world, and never has been. It's just that now, non-binary people have found their voices and are less afraid to speak up. Language takes a while to catch up to culture, and the wheels grind slow. Still, the grammar part still applies to me, so I'll leave it here and hope to be forgiven.

I guess I'm just old-fashioned. I learned to use he, him, and his to mean persons in general, and I find the alternatives clunky. Therefore, whether I've been successful at updating my grammar or not, parents of daughters, be assured that I mean your child too. As the mother of a boy and a girl, I know that what I've written applies equally to both. And should you or your child be someone yet to decide, or one who rejects all things binary, be assured everything in life applies to you too. Respect, trust, and a listening ear are due all.

Introduction to The Second Edition

by Marian Tompson, Founding Mother, La Leche League

Do we need yet another book telling us how to raise our children? Aren't parents already confused enough by the ever-multiplying array of treatises aimed at helping them produce near perfect children who grow up to be competent adults? This dilemma was recently illustrated in the nationally syndicated comic strip, Rose is Rose. In the first panel of the strip we see Rose and her friend, Abby, pushing strollers down the street, deep in conversation. "If you ask me, Abby, you should just do your best with Mimi and not worry so much about what others think!" Rose is saying. The need for this reassurance becomes quickly obvious in the next panel as the mothers walk by and we can see lettered on the back of Abby's jacket the plaintive plea, "How's my mothering? Call toll free 1-800-555-2573."

Being a parent has never been easy, but today it seems like the whole world is watching what we do. Within our own neighborhood or circle of friends there might be strong disagreement over parenting approaches. Should we give birth to our baby in the hospital or at home? Should we breast-feed, and if we do, for how long? Does it make a difference if someone else raises our children? Do we send them to public school, private school, or educate them ourselves at home? And too often, engrossed in the intense concentration necessary for making the "right" decision, we miss out on much of the poetry, the music, and "joie de vivre" that is also part of being a parent. Weighed down by the responsibility of sifting through conflicting opinions, we tend to forget that simply tuning in to our own baby will often give us answers more suitable to that particular child's needs than listening to most outsiders. And even the advice of experts, scientific as it may sound, reflects, in some way, their own experience as children and as parents.

Years ago when La Leche began we were puzzled by one young mother who continued to come to meetings long after she had weaned her baby. When we finally asked Lorraine what she was getting out of the discussions, she told us that it had nothing to do with breast-feeding but that "you women so obviously enjoy your children that I hope by hanging around, some of your enjoyment of motherhood will rub off on me."

INSPIRING PARENTHOOD is written by a woman who enjoys being a mother. I've known Janice Presser for a long time and in this book she speaks from her heart, sharing the wisdom she has gained as a mother and as a therapist working with other families. She is the next-door neighbor everyone would like to have, quick to see the humor in life, yet sensitive to the fears and worries that beset all of us at some time.

Janice knows that babies are meant to inspire us and to bring out our noblest behavior. As parents, we provide the security and nurturing that enables babies to become all that they are capable of being. While children teach us what life is all about, it is through our fidelity and commitment that they come to understand the true meaning of love.

In acknowledging this emotional and spiritual dimension, INSPIRING PARENTHOOD goes beyond the advice offered in most books on childcare and in doing so takes us straight to the heart of what being a family is all about.

Marian Tompson,
co-founder La Leche League International

(Update note by the author: It is with my delight, that these many years later, Marian still feels this way. Though the intervening years have brought us far apart geographically, we still share our fundamental belief in the sanctity of parenthood and our mutual desire to support those who undertake the challenges that parents in these uncertain times deserve.)

A Few Notes
on the Third Edition

It seems like a lifetime ago when I first wrote this book. With children still in school, I was between my masters and doctorate, had just closed a family business, and was working as a nurse/counselor in a mental health crisis unit. It was a hectic time.

Four years later the second edition came out. I had finished my doctorate, was working as a family therapist and teaching college courses, planning my next book, and waiting for our last little bird to fly out of the nest.

Between then and now there were more changes than I ever would have thought possible. Still, the core of life is the same. In the technology company I founded in 2001, we'd say that core is "trust, respect, and faith" no matter what you are trying to accomplish. Whether you are at work or at home, living with trust, acting with respect, and being of faith will ground you to what is important in life. And the beneficiaries will be your children and all the children of the future.

So be assured that this is not a massive rewrite of either the first or second edition. Some things have been updated, like the price of food, since they really have changed. Others have been marveled over and left just as they were written. It is good to know that your deepest beliefs are eternally true.

One other update, though, which is long overdue.

This edition is dedicated to the memory of Margot Pordes, who left this earth too soon, and is doubtless now organizing bands of angels to do whatever is needed to keep Heaven running well. She was my best friend, comadre, and sister-in-spirit.

As young mothers, we fought for the rights of women to nurse their babies on their own schedule, for the rights to birth them as nature intended, and for the protection of those who others often failed to protect. As we grew, so did our mutual scope of concern for injustice and inequity. I miss her dearly.

J.P.
January 1, 2019

Preparing

Inspiring Parenthood begins long before marriage. It begins in our own childhood, in the learning environment of the family, for it is then that the feelings and attitudes about marriage and parenting are born. If we were lucky enough to be brought up in a loving family, where our parents used just the right balance of firm guidance and respect for our independence, self-confidence and belief in our innate ability to be marital partners and parents come naturally. For those who had cold or aloof parents, whose discipline was overly harsh or nonexistent, or whose parents never demonstrated affection or joy, selecting a partner and learning to be a parent may be very difficult tasks. Some people are unable even to attempt these things.

A couple's marital relationship shapes its reactions to parenthood: if our parents were satisfied with each other, their cooperation and mutual goals would allow them to divide family responsibilities easily. Mother would be the bearer and nurturer of the young, while Father would be the provider and protector, insuring that all children born to the marriage had the best chance of flourishing—not merely surviving—to adulthood.

Taking pleasure in her biologically dictated role would not eliminate all other career possibilities for the mother, of course, but her satisfaction with mothering—her belief that it is a divine blessing—would be transmitted to her children. Likewise, a father who feels pride in his wife's ability to mother his children and who feels that they are involved in a mutual project, with God's help, passes on the desire to be a father to his sons.

In addition, the schools we attend, the religious and social groups we belong to, and the media we are exposed to all temper our childhood feelings and attitudes. As recently as thirty years ago, our media characters were family-oriented, providing us with idealized role models of families, where there was always enough time, always enough space, always enough money, and, likely as not, a faithful family retainer to ensure that no two family members bickered over whose turn it was to take out the trash. The new (third wave!) feminist movement may decry these old series as being insulting to women who want more out of life than a clean apron, but they are still available on independent stations and multiple streaming platforms so someone's listening. Even Michelle Obama said it, in response to the idea that all women have to do is 'lean in' and grab it. As the former First Lady recently opined, you can't have it all.

Perhaps this indicates a backlash of those who are tired of the largely antimarriage, anti-parenthood media messages that have left many potential parents questioning their natural inclinations.

Yet despite the antifamily Cassandras who proclaim that marriage is dead and who eagerly await the era when test tubes will be used for gestation as well as conception, most people still want to fall in love, marry, and have children. Lacking a set of guidelines for success, they may marry for physical attraction and then wonder why the storybook marriage is not living up to its promise of "happily ever after." The problem is usually not with one member of the couple; rather, it is the expectations each has of the other and of their marriage. These expectations may be as mundane as the woman expecting the man to know how to relight the furnace (because her father did, of course) or as serious as his expectation that she will stay home when the children are small (his mother did, of course).

Expectations are like a hidden, secret language that each partner has learned early in life. No two people have exactly the same expectations, so no two 'languages' are exactly the same. Opposites may attract, but one of the reasons that marriages between those with similar backgrounds often last longer is simply that the more similar the upbringing of the couple, the closer their language of expectations is likely to be. Old-fashioned courting rituals, currently making a comeback along with tighter parental controls on teenage behavior, served as a kind of tutoring in one's private language.

Since many couples do come from dissimilar cultural, economic, and social backgrounds, it can be helpful to come up with mutual definitions of love, marriage, parenting, and so on. Differences do not mean that a relationship will not be successful, only that there may be a greater need for compromise and the creation of a new language.

It is difficult to put into words that which philosophers and poets have always struggled with. Assessing your feelings and expectations can be done through nonverbal means, such as drawing and miming. For instance, one way to look at some different styles of marriage is to symbolize the couple as eggs.

Some couples are like hard-boiled eggs. They're firm and well done, but they can't get very close to each other. They may shatter each other's shell, but even that just brings their outer beings (the white part) together. Their inner selves (the yolks) are isolated from each other. The hard-boiled-egg couples have what's termed a "marriage of convenience." No risk; little intimacy.

Other couples are like soft-boiled eggs. One healthy confrontation and they're a messy puddle, impossible to put back together for a bit more cooking. Very young couples, especially those who have been forced to marry because of untimely pregnancies, are often soft-boiled egg couples. High-risk; intimacy only when the inner selves are shattered.

Then there are the scrambled eggs. They have even given up their uniqueness to create a single, homogenized entity. They may have a feeling of "us against the world," but it is a false feeling of security, since neither can function well alone. If there are children, they, too, may be expected to become part of the omelet, submerging themselves in the family. Low-risk for the couple; high risk for their children; and a largely false sense of intimacy.

Successful couples are like fried eggs, sunny-side up. When they are cracked open against the side of the pan, they obligingly plop in, their outer selves attracted to each other, coming together to form a mutual environment for the two yolks. The yolks may move around in their white field, sometimes touching and sometimes moving apart, yet they always retain their individuality. They risk moving against each other with enough force to break one or both, but their mutual base tends to slow down any confrontation. Their intimacy has room for additional little eggs; children are no major threat, since there is space for them to develop as individuals too. Acceptable risk; high probability of intimacy; and personal growth is enabled for all.

To carry the egg analogy a bit further, it should be noted that each member of the couple carries along a prefabricated environment, the white part. This includes each one's own family, career, social and economic situation, friendships, obligations, assets and liabilities. Religious values and ethics, learned since childhood, may be similar or not. Each member of the couple may attach more or less importance to the same aspect of the personal environment. For instance, to one, career may be the main source of confirmation of worth in this world, while to the other working is just a way to maintain life's necessities while devoting the 'living' to family or charitable pursuits. The conflicts are most evident when dealing with one of the three finite resources: time, space, and money. When two lives are spent in the same frying pan, there is bound to be some relocation that leaves one or both members feeling cheated.

Those who believe they can prevent time from moving on, who are determined to work twenty-five hours a day, who never stop to really see the snowflakes, may need to look inward to find the source of their rushing about, preferably before they attempt to marry and become parents. Often these overly busy folks find it intolerable to live with a slower-moving person, and equally intolerable to live with someone who may occasionally surpass their activity level. When children enter the picture and radical surgery has to be done on both partners' busy schedules, the rusharound may decline to participate, preferring instead to be the supplier of money and objects, but not really being involved in a personal way.

One way of predicting what effect marriage and ultimately parenthood will have on a couple is to analyze how they spend their time and if they plan any changes.

A simple method is to make up a calendar of a typical week, showing the seven days across the top and the twenty-four hours down the side. Then the couple blocks out the time they have committed to work (paid and volunteer, including travel time), sleeping, eating, and personal hygiene, other priorities and/or obligations (church attendance, visiting elderly family members, etc.), and finally "free" time. By comparing their charts, the couple can see at a glance where potential conflicts may lie. For instance, one member may be clearing out vast time blocks to be able to have more contact with the other, while that partner believes that life will go on as before and that marriage should not interfere with one's personal pursuit of pleasure.

The graphic representation of how the partners expect to pass their life together forces them to acknowledge and, hopefully, to resolve their differences. Requiring each other to define and redefine life priorities is a necessary prerequisite for having children, since the addition of a baby creates the need for even more redefinition and resolution.

Space allocation is another subject for potential conflicts, especially if one member of the couple likes to spread out and the other prefers to condense. The cliché fights over the toothpaste tube (cap on or off) are often symbolic of an overall space conflict, the open toothpaste being perceived as a more rational thing to argue about than the piles of dirty laundry growing on one or both sides of the bed. One can argue that the uncapped tube is wasteful, since the toothpaste dries up and needs to be replaced more often, but one's complaints of the other's sloppiness can easily deteriorate into name- calling, whining, or nagging.

There is no magical immunization against marital conflict, but consistently attempting to resolve conflicts in mutually acceptable ways can keep them to a survivable minimum. As with time, space analysis starts with both partners diagramming their living quarters and, with different colors, filling in the spaces that are allocated to each and what is considered 'ours.' If there are already children, their space should be noted too. If there's a baby on the way, a brief trip to the baby department or specialty store can provide the information necessary to figure out exactly how much room the little one is going to absorb. As with time, the allocation of space doesn't have to be equal (hopefully, adults have learned that life isn't "fair") but can be traded off with the other finite resources. For instance, her hobby is bowling; his is playing his grand piano. He requires more room; she needs a few hours away from home. Solution: they schedule deliveries and repair visits while he's practicing sonatas and she's making splits.

Money is another matter entirely; technically, it may be finite (at any given time, assets add up to a finite number) but in actual use, one can get more or less out of every dollar, depending on how finicky a shopper one is. The other complicating factor is that money has more than its practical value: it is also a symbol in our society of success. For many people, the higher the number on their paycheck, the more successful they feel in comparison to others.

Before marriage, most couples don't plan how they will manage their money. They usually slide into one of the standard methods: they either pool their funds and the more mathematically inclined member balances the checkbook and doles out an allowance to the other, or they each manage their money separately, sharing the major expenses and assuming that everything will even out in the end. The first method works well for traditional couples, where the wife is expected to stay home with the children and forgo a career and the husband agrees to support the family. If they take their marriage vows seriously and there is no threat of divorce, and both enter into the agreement fully aware that each is giving up some options in favor of the life-style they have freely chosen, this mode of family life can work well as it has for countless generations.

The second method, in which the couple attempts to be "fair," by contributing proportionately to their incomes, often deteriorates into two separate people each trying to determine which one is getting the better bargain. It's a method well suited to a marriage of convenience, but not to those who believe that each partner should contribute one hundred percent. Still, with planning, any method that both partners freely agree to can work out well.

Having a baby changes the balance of financial power in couples who view their relative economic contribution to the marriage as indicative of the power they wield. If the mother stays home to raise the child, her income falls to zero; her relative worth as an individual soars (whether she and society recognize it or not). Unless some rearrangement of resources is made, the new mother can begin to feel trapped—or even experience a severe loss of self-esteem—even though she truly wants to be a fulltime mother. This is true also, where the other parent takes over the 'day shift' of childcare.

Two people who feel that their being together is a priceless gift, a divine confirmation of their individual worth, will invariably find it easier to adapt to sharing their assets than the couple that stays together largely because they are afraid to consider that they might be happier apart. The inspired couple feels fulfilled, literally filled by each other's gift of love; material pleasures pale in comparison. Still, there are practical ways to minimize the petty frictions that can erode even the most steadfast relationship.

A home economics planning session should include discussion of the following:

Goals: What do we want to save for? How much should we put away each pay period? How shall we invest our surplus?

Security: How much (if any) insurance do we want? Do we need to make wills? Plan for potential disasters?

Accounting: How will we accomplish the money management tasks like balancing the checkbook (joint? individual?) and doing taxes?

Responsibility: How will we communicate budget decisions to each other? What dollar amount shall we set as the limit we want to have for expenditures that don't require the other's consent ($10? $50? $100? More?)

It's relatively easy to assess these finite areas of life. Far more complicated is analyzing the spiritual quality of life as a couple and as prospective parents.

Yet this is the time, before the marriage vows are spoken, to face the issues that will affect you as marital partners and parents. Attitudes about child-rearing may seem extraneous when all your attention is focused on wedding plans and honeymoon resorts, but time has a way of passing quietly by those who say they'll think about things tomorrow. Of course, if your children are already born, it's not too late to talk things out. Still, it is comforting to know that you are both headed in the same direction before you start your journey together.

Simplistic as it may sound, the basis of successful marital life is love. More than just sexual attraction, more than friendship, a happy marriage requires love in all its manifestations. This love encompasses love of the self, of the creatures of the earth and their Creator, and of the loved one as friend, partner, co-parent, and lover. This love is limitless, expanding to embrace the growth and development of the loved one, friends, and family members. This is love that asks "How can I help you?" rather than "What do you want from me now?" This love acknowledges the other person's need for room to breathe, to dream, to wonder, to question.

To those raised with the idea that love of the self leads only to selfish behavior, it may seem peculiar that self-love is a necessary prerequisite to mature partnership-for-life love. But remember the admonition to "love thy neighbor as thyself"; if the self is not deemed lovable, how can one then love another being? Love that asks for the sacrifice of the self is not love but some perversion, as in the Faust legend, where Mephistopheles (the devil) asks for the sacrifice of the self (Faust's soul) in exchange for material gifts. A loving God gives life and love that nurtures the soul. Inspiring parents re-create that soul-nurturing environment for their children, appreciating each one's individuality and innate goodness. In turn, the grace of their love is reflected back on them, filling and refilling the wellspring of their souls.

Loving thy neighbor means more than merely being kind to the family next door. It extends to all creatures, since all were created by God and are therefore all worthy of care and respect. What many couples forget over their years of marriage is that they should also treat each other with this loving respect. The expression "Charity begins at home" is used more often as an excuse for ignoring the other creatures than as an excellent standard. Charity is not just pennies in a collection plate and a check hastily scrawled to the local cancer care group. Rather, it is love, generosity, affection, goodwill to all, and its exercise toward all can only enhance our ability to be charitable toward those we are closest to.

Love of God is expressed in many ways, from community prayer meetings to the solitary experience of being overwhelmed by reverence at the sight of a magnificent sunrise. The method of worship may be an area of conflict for the couple which needs to be resolved before there are children; regardless, both need to feel that they will be able to continue to express their deepest religious feelings in their own way.

If childhood religions are radically different, a couple may need to consider if their attraction to each other is a kind of rebellion against their parents. Mature love allows for difference and compromise: some couples, realizing that it is the worship of God that is central to all religions, choose to join a new faith community that is mutually acceptable and meets their spiritual and relational needs.

If each chooses to retain his individual religious affiliation, it is crucial to discuss and decide how children will be raised in terms of religious education. Very little is more confusing to a child than to be raised in an environment where each parent is convinced that his or her faith is the only acceptable or "right" one. When that happens, the child is forced to deal with the possibility that only one parent will "go to heaven."

Loving each other as friends requires that you really enjoy your life together. Having a mutual interest enhances a friendship (unless it becomes a focus for competition), but sometimes the best of friends are attracted because of their passions for dissimilar activities. Love is a wonderful reason for learning to play tennis or identify wild birds.

Being lovers to each other, with the implied physical and spiritual intimacy, is seen by many as independent of the other forms of love felt by the couple. But erotic love requires the same respect of the other as friendship and charity do, and without self-love, erotic love is impossible. The commitment to love, in its fullest sense, is what makes the marital union complete. The feeling of being partners, and at the same time individuals and part of a unity, brings the most exquisite joy and tenderness to marital love.

Finally, couples need to love each other as co-parents. Although most child-care books stress the need of the child for loving care by one or more parents or substitute caretakers, most ignore the need the child has for parents who are partners, loving each other, their children, their Supreme Being, with humility and joy. Babies are often looked on as total solipsists, aware of no one but themselves and of no feelings but their own, but they are far more sensitive to the subtleties of the environment than formerly acknowledged.

Babies need parents who are both inspired and inspiring: inspired by their awareness of their connection to each other and God and wanting to reflect that inspiration onto their offspring, creating a family environment of love and joy. No matter how big the family grows, parents need to grow with their family, reproducing and regenerating the ecstasy and rapture of love.

Prepare us to receive Your blessing of parenthood with devotion and joy.

Show us the way to patience and forbearance, for ourselves as well as each other, for family as well as strangers.

Shield our love for each other from pettiness and scorn; help us recognize the source of our annoyance so that we may dissolve it with kindness.

Help us create a quiet place in our marriage, the center of our two souls, where we can be alone together with You.

When we feel prideful and arrogant, remind us gently of our humanity, and forgive us our shortcomings.

Teach us to see each other clearly but let us never lose the vision we have of each other in this moment, wreathed in the sanctity of Your love, joyous in this meeting.

BEGINNING

The purpose of mating is the propagation of the species. Plants pollinate, creating random encounters of male and female; many lower-order creatures lay eggs, which are then fertilized by whichever male of the species reaches them first; and those, like dogs and cats, with estrus cycles ("heat") emit special mating odors, which signal that the female is fertile and sexually receptive. All these modes of reproduction fulfill God's commandment to "go forth and multiply." Only the mating of human beings is graced with further purpose than mere propagation.

The human family exists to protect and socialize the offspring, to nurture their souls in the medium of loving guidance. Left to themselves, provided only with food and shelter, some children would grow to maturity, though the vast majority would die in infancy without nurturing. Numerous studies of orphanages and infant hospitals have shown that lack of love leads to infantile depression ("marasmus"), a disease characterized by wasting away, dying of if not a broken heart, then certainly one that has been badly damaged.

To increase the chances that a newborn will be wanted and cared for, women have greater control over reproduction than do daisies, goldfish, or pandas. Voluntary sexual encounters generally take place between two adults who know and trust each other, with full awareness of the consequences of fertility. For those who are ready and eager to become parents, fertility is a blessing rather than an obstacle to enjoyment.

With all the publicity given to test-tube babies, reversible sterilization operations, surrogate motherhood, and new, improved birth control methods, most couples make the false assumption that fertility is easily turned on and off. But though chemists and surgeons may perfect their arts and inventions, the ultimate control of fertility is not in human hands. Fertility is rhythmic but trying to make its rhythm synchronize with some outside force may only cause us to lose the beat and miss hearing the divine melody. (Now understand, I am not lobbying against planned parenthood in any way, but only trying to expand the limited amount of knowledge we all gather from our primary sources, increasingly the ads on our social media platforms.)

Hormonal forms of birth control try to fool the woma1an's body into thinking that it is pregnant. This subterfuge works for most women, although there is a small minority for whom pregnancy occurs despite the faithful use of the pill. Perhaps their bodies are more sensitive than they are given credit for, or perhaps the unconscious desire for parenthood is more prevalent than is assumed. The same is true of the intrauterine devices (IUDs), which work by creating a low-grade chronic inflammation in the uterus that generally acts to prevent the continuation of pregnancy past the first week. Some "accidents" (though it is difficult to consider a baby an accident) are due to the mother's taking antibiotics for another infection: the antibiotics also work to clear the uterine inflammation, potentially restoring fertility. In other cases, the pregnancy may just represent the triumph of life over technology.

Rather than trying to fight fertility, more and more couples are choosing to fall into step with its rhythms. Instead of using contraceptives that may have long-range side effects, such as total loss of fertility, they choose to be responsible lovers, inspired rather than frightened and disgusted by their bodies. They actively select natural family planning rather than passively accept the sociologists' and politicians' notions of population control.

Natural family planning starts with the couple learning about their bodies' own rhythms. Unlike the simpler forms of the "rhythm method," where all one does is count the days and abstain from intercourse during the days of average highest fertility, natural family planning considers individual differences both between people and within the many cycles of their lives. In order to understand how it works, the couple first needs to understand how the processes of sperm production, ovulation, and conception work. I'll try not to sound too pedantic, but I've got an additional purpose here. Understanding the basics will give you confidence when you eventually have to pass the information on to your children and don't want them to tell you they'll just look it up on the internet.

Sperm production takes place within the man's testes. There, primitive cells replicate themselves over and over again from puberty until the end of life. Some of these newly replicated cells continue to mature by separating into two equal cells, each with half the original genetic material, which, of course, has the same genetic makeup as the man. Since just about all men carry one X chromosome and one Y chromosome (besides the twenty-two pairs of chromosomes that determine characteristics other than gender), half the resultant sperm cells will produce females, and half males. (I say 'just about' because, although most people identified at birth as males are XY, as most females are XX, there are rare exceptions.) It seems that the more science learns about gender, the more interesting things get, but I'll leave that for another book and go with the majority here. So, since women—who have two X chromosomes—can contribute only an X chromosome, it is the man's contribution that determines the gender of the child. Finally, each secondary sperm cell replicates itself, and the resultant spermatids are ready to grow into mature sperm.

The spermatids are nourished in the testes until they are ready to make the long trip to the egg. During sexual arousal, the sperm travel past glands that secrete the other components of semen. Just before orgasm, a lubricant is secreted that speeds the sperm on the trip through the urethra on the way to the woman's uterus and, eventually, toward the ovum.

The journey is rather straightforward; there are relatively few things that can go wrong. Rarely, there is a total absence of sperm. More frequently there may be a lowered sperm count, which is often a temporary condition due to an infection somewhere in the body (even a dental problem may lower fertility) or an environmental condition, such as working in a very high temperature or wearing clothing that holds the scrotum tightly against the body. This is because the optimum temperature for sperm production is about 94 degrees Fahrenheit, several degrees cooler than the usual body temperature of somewhere between 96 and 98.6 degrees Fahrenheit. (It seems that as old data is reexamined, scientists agree less!) Medications, illnesses, and emotional stress have also been implicated in lowered sperm counts, though many of these situations are temporary and attempting to correct a normal, temporary situation may result in unnecessary complications. Perhaps temporary lowered fertility is God's way of discouraging pregnancy and parenthood at a time when a baby might be perceived as creating more stress than the marriage can survive.

Female fertility is more complicated, since it involves more than just the production of the ovum; not only must the ovum be well developed, but the transport mechanisms must be timed to coincide with the lushest growth phase of the uterine lining. Additionally, the environment must not be hostile to the entering sperm, and after fertilization, which takes place in the woman's oviduct (also called the Fallopian tube), the newly conceived baby must remain small enough to continue to fit through the very narrow opening of the tube on its way to the uterus.

Female fertility starts with the ovum: all the eggs a woman will ever have are present in her tiny ovaries before she is even born. Starting with puberty, each month about a thousand of the ova begin to mature; generally, only one matures fully and is released from the ovary, while the others stop developing. (If more than one egg is released and fertilized the woman may become pregnant with fraternal twins. These babies will share the prenatal environment but will come from different eggs and different sperm, so they will look as much alike as or as different from each other as any other two siblings. They may, of course, be male, female, or one of each. More rarely, there may be fraternal triplets, quadruplets, or more.) The ovum develops within a bubblelike chamber on the ovary called a follicle.

Hormones cause the ovum to bulge out from the follicle,

finally erupting from the surface and entering the oviduct. The empty follicle begins to produce a pro-gestation hormone, progesterone, which causes the cervix (entryway to the uterus) to become impermeable, as if to protect the life growing within. The progesterone also softens the lush growth of the uterine lining, creating the optimal consistency for implantation of the fertilized ovum. But conception requires more than just a healthy ovum and abundant sperm. Although couples may enjoy their intimate relationship at all times of the cycle, conception is actually possible only during the ovum's life span, thought to be about six hours.

Sexual expression is a powerful human bond. So powerful, in fact, that to limit it to just that short time of every monthly cycle would be detrimental to the idea of human offspring being raised by two parents. Human beings are, therefore, sexually receptive at all times during the cycle. This desire strengthens the marital bond, but in order to prevent conception at a time when the ovum is too old or the uterine lining not quite right, the uterus is cooperative only during the forty-eight hours preceding ovulation.

When ejaculation (the male orgasm) takes place during other times of the cycle, the sperm meet a closed door. The cervix is filled with thick, impenetrable mucus. But near the time of ovulation, the cervical mucus gets soft and stretchy, a condition that aids the sperm on the first step of their journey. Couples who practice natural family planning can use this mucus sign as a clue to the time of highest fertility. It's done with a touch of a finger to her cervix, then a quick touch of that finger to the thumb, then a quick separation of finger and thumb. If the cervical mucus forms an elastic string, ovulation is about to occur. (At other times the string is shorter and less elastic.) New practitioners of natural family planning need to compare mucus samples at several times during the month to learn to recognize this sign, which is called "spinnbarkheit." To maximize the chance of conception, the couple should have intercourse twenty-four to forty-eight hours before ovulation.

When intercourse takes place during this time, the cervix is most receptive, although, of course conception is never guaranteed. Of the three to four hundred million sperm in the average ejaculate, only about one hundred thousand get through the cervix. Most are lost in other areas of the vagina, too far away from the cervix, while others die in the attempt to penetrate the cervical mucus. The sperm that follow those who die in "front-line action" have the best chance of getting to the ovum. The difficult journey insures that only the strongest, healthiest sperm will survive. Once the sperm enter the uterus, they must move toward the mouth of the oviduct, which contains the ovum (rarely will there be an ovum in each, in which case, the chance of fraternal twins goes up). Of the one hundred thousand sperm that pass the cervical barrier, only about four hundred will reach the oviduct, and of those only about forty, the hardiest warriors, will reach the ovum. If the timing is right, the egg will be fresh and the sperm vigorous. The sperm swim around the ovum, attempting to penetrate the jelly surrounding it with the help of chemicals released by their spear-shaped tips, until finally one is successful. At that moment the membranes of both sperm and ovum form a boundary against the invasion of the other sperm, preventing the fertilization of the ovum by more than one sperm, which would add up to too many chromosomes. A new life is begun.

If life begins with conception, so then does parenting. At the very moment that two unique elements of life—the man's sperm and the woman's ovum—unite, a new individual is formed, identical to neither parent nor to any other being who has lived before. This new life is more than the sum of sperm and ovum; the act of fertilization creates a cell that will reproduce, from its simple components, life in all its diverse glory.

The cells duplicate their genetic material and reproduce themselves repeatedly, forming a tiny berry-shaped mass while traveling down the oviduct toward the uterus. Within a week of fertilization, the new being is putting down roots in the prenatal environment. Burrowing softly into the spongy inner layer of the mother's uterus, which lies protected in the cradle of her pelvic bone structure, the baby instinctively seeks nourishment. The burrowing action creates a pool of nutrients, courtesy of the mother's bloodstream, for the baby's special organ, the placenta, to grow in. As the baby grows, the placenta will also grow, providing more surface area for the exchange of nutrients for the baby's waste products, much as an adult's lungs exchange oxygen for carbon dioxide in the blood. But the placenta is more than just a gas exchanger: everything the mother ingests, whether willingly or unwillingly, healthful or not, will reach the baby via the placenta.

From that point of implantation until birth, some nine months later, mother and baby form a unique dual organism. The baby is not a parasite, as was previously believed (a parasite is an organism that depends on an organism of other species for sustenance) but is part of an interdependent system. The baby does not "feed off" the mother, although it does share the nutrients she takes in. If she does not supply enough to feed both her and her baby, the baby will suffer. If she is in an accident and loses a large amount of blood, she may well miscarry as the placenta is deprived of blood in favor of her vital organs.

Mother and baby are separate; their bloodstreams do not mix, even though nutritional and waste components are exchanged. They are individuals, with separate and often very different styles (just ask the very placid pregnant woman whose baby seems to be practicing to be a gymnast while still occupying her uterus!). However, they are interdependent. If the mother's nutritional intake is inadequate to support the growth of her baby, the pregnancy may terminate in a complication that is fatal to the baby and life-threatening or even fatal to her. Thus, insuring the well-being of the mother insures the wellbeing of the baby, and vice versa. If the mother takes care of herself physically, nutritionally, emotionally, and spiritually, the baby thrives; the mother who abuses herself by consuming unnecessary drugs (including alcohol), by dieting, by allowing herself to be exposed to hazardous chemicals and pollutants, or by not limiting the stress in her life to a manageable level can hurt herself and the growing baby.

The effects of smoking have been well publicized (the carbon monoxide in the smoke binds the hemoglobin in the mother's blood, reducing the amount of oxygen available to the baby, resulting in slower growth and lower birth weight), as have the effects of alcohol (the "fetal alcohol syndrome" is a set of deformities that appears with unacceptable frequency among the infants of heavy, even sporadically heavy, drinkers). Less well known is the fact that many drugs, those prescribed by physicians as well as the illegal variety, can also be damaging. (The scientific term is "teratogenic," from the Greek meaning monster-forming). Because drugs may affect the genetic blueprint, rewriting some of the biological specifications encoded in the chromosomes, normal fetal development goes awry, resulting in varying degrees of abnormality, depending on the age of the unborn baby at the time the drug is taken.

Although there are no guarantees that a baby will be physically perfect, there are ways to nurture your baby before birth. First is to search your lives for potentially harmful habits, ideally before conception occurs. Smoking, drinking, unnecessary drugs, and ignoring inner needs for peace and joy are counterproductive; they may even interfere with fertility.

Second is to provide the baby with all the nutrients necessary for full growth and development. This is accomplished simply by feeding the mother every day with foods from the Lord's glorious bounty: a quart of milk, two eggs, two large servings of protein-rich food (meat, poultry, fish, or vegetarian combinations), five servings of whole grains, two servings of citrus or other high vitamin C produce (tomatoes, peppers, potatoes, cabbage), three servings of bright yellow or green vegetables or fruits, some fats and oils, and salt to taste and water to thirst. Satisfying the mother's appetite with these natural gifts leaves little room for nutritionally empty, artificially produced, chemical-laden "foods." Also, by learning to associate eating well with nurturing the baby, she is likely to eat more of these good foods if she is still hungry rather than attempt to control her weight by limiting the foods she shares with her growing child. (A larger appetite can be a clue that the "baby" may in fact be "babies"!)

The third way to nurture the unborn baby is to get the kind of exercise that nurtures the pregnant woman's body. Although many women athletes continue to train throughout pregnancy, claiming that the vigorous exercise gives them easier labors and births, there are some reasons for foregoing excessive body training during the childbearing years.

A certain amount of fat is necessary for the production of hormones, so women whose percentage of body fat dips below a certain level often cease to ovulate and are actually sterile. While this may be seen as an advantage by a sexually active woman who does not want to become pregnant, her situation and desires may change. Having become used to her very trim body (much like an adolescent male's), she may be reluctant to slow down and put back the pounds that will cause her to ovulate once again and may instead be treated for her "infertility" with potentially hazardous drugs.

During pregnancy the woman athlete may eat well, but the vigorous exercising may use up so many calories that her baby is deprived. In addition, working out usually causes the body temperature to rise, and such temperature elevations (as well as those from saunas, hot tubs, and working in torrid environments) have been shown to increase the possibility of fetal malformation.

The best exercise for pregnancy is walking and talking, together. Thus, exercise becomes part of the nurturance of the spirit of the family. The couple adjusts to each other's pace (a curious idea to the competition-minded but far more valuable a lesson in human relations) while providing a rhythmically rocking cradle for the baby within. Without housework, careers, smart phones, or television, there is only each other to focus on.

As with nutrition and exercise, what benefits the mother in a spiritual sense also nurtures the baby. Biochemists have shown that in stressful situations, where people feel powerless over their own lives, there are large shifts in the blood levels of some body chemicals. Since the components of the mother's blood are available to the baby and are not selectively screened as previously thought (the placenta used to be called the "placental barrier" until it was realized that just about any molecule could get through), it is reasonable to assume that when the mother is stressed, so is the baby. While small amounts of stress help us learn to deal with the hard times, repeated large doses are wearing.

Stress management begins with the acceptance that life is often difficult. The couple's commitment to each other and to the family they hope to have help to make that acceptance easier. Knowing that in good times and in hard times they are not alone but are at one in spirit with their God forms the basis for their future life together.

Graced with fertile ground,
Receptive to our rhythms,
We wait.
Nourished by each other,
Harbored in Your solace,
We prepare.
Thankful for Your guidance,
Hopeful of Your blessing,
We trust.
Awed by the power,
Inspired by the glory,
We pray.

Awaiting

The moment when a long-awaited conception is confirmed is a moment of truth. Feelings surface at this time: joy for the new life, pride in one's body's ability to create, relief that the great event has finally happened, and perhaps some ambivalence or second thoughts. The nine long months that follow are not only for nurturing the baby to the point that life outside is possible: the parents, too, need that time for growing in grace.

Throughout the pregnancy, new situations and issues challenge the couple physically, emotionally, spiritually. Meeting the challenges, feeling your confidence grow in your ability to be parents to the unborn child, prepares you for the even greater challenges of caring for the newborn, the toddler, the preschooler, the child reaching toward adolescence, toward adulthood. Meeting the challenges together, one in the spirit, opens the couple to the full cycle of parenthood.

The early months of pregnancy are marked by the rapid physical changes in the mother's body that, at the same time, alter her internal environment and prepare her for feeding the baby after birth. There is no denying that these body changes do cause varying degrees of discomfort in some women but understanding the purpose of the changes should neutralize any feeling that pregnancy is a sacrificial act. Growing pains are part of growth, for parents as well as children.

The most common discomfort of early pregnancy is nausea—'morning sickness' though it is just as likely to happen in the evening. Some women are frightened by the feeling, associating it with illness, but it is merely a bodily response to the extra stimulation of pregnancy hormones on the digestive system. On a more positive note, these feelings, along with the other intestinal complaints, such as constipation, gas, and heartburn, serve to help the mother tune in to her body sensations and to become aware of what works to make her feel better. Rather than moan and groan, perhaps taking to bed, it's helpful to accept these transitory discomforts as normal. This makes it easier to think about ways to relieve them, just as later parents have to accept the pain of their newborn's discomforts and will strive to correct them rather than indulge in their painful responses (listening to your baby cry, parents discover, is far more painful than dealing with a bout of nausea!)

For many women, pregnancy is the first time in their lives that they need to consider the quality of food that they eat. The working, childless woman, generally less home-centered than the mother, easily becomes acclimated to fast-food breakfasts (or coffee and pastry from the snack wagon or conference room), business lunches (with or without alcohol, often heavy and lacking fiber to keep her digestive system in good working order), and take-out dinners. Scheduled by the appointment book instead of by internal needs, people often eat when they are not hungry, eat what they neither savor nor recognize as being nutritious, and eat under stress or time pressure. No wonder the pregnant woman's stomach rebels when another being is crying for some nutritional consideration!

With the baby so close to the digestive system, as the months progress the mother feels fuller on smaller amounts of food. Since the baby needs more food rather than less, the sensitive mother just needs to eat more frequently, making each meal smaller. Mothers carrying more than one child often find that in the latter months they do little more than eat (more babies means more nutrients needed) and sleep!

Halfway through the pregnancy the mother's body has generally adjusted to the presence of the child and the nausea abates. As her midsection blossoms, making accommodating clothing necessary, a new peace envelops the mother. She is "officially pregnant," a member of that exclusive club that used to be called "ladies-in-waiting." While her grandmother may have hidden her condition, embarrassed by the tacit admission of her sexuality, most modern women are pleased by the acknowledgment of their womanliness and proudly post pictures of the 'baby bump.' Even very weight-conscious women who may feel vaguely uneasy about the growing bulge ("Is it really a baby, or have I eaten something I shouldn't have?") are usually pleased by one growing area: her breasts.

In the well-nourished pregnant woman, hormones produced by the placenta cause her breasts to tingle with activity. The grapelike clusters of milk ducts grow and multiply while the blood flow through the new capillaries makes the breasts feel warm and full. All this is in preparation for the moment of birth, the moment when the baby will no longer be fed by the nutrients of the mother's bloodstream traveling via the placenta but will need a new connection to the mother to insure survival. All the needs that before birth were met by the mother's body—the needs for food, for warmth, for enveloping embrace, for external sensations—will from then on be met by the grace of breast-feeding. The same attention to the baby, through nutrition with love, readies the mother's body to meet this challenge.

Breast-feeding is more than just a way for the mother to provide nutrition after birth; it guides her gently into the realization of her role as mother. Breast-feeding necessitates holding the baby (since it's impossible to 'prop' a breast or leave one with a baby-sitter) in an enfolding embrace. No mother has to learn how to hold a baby to provide this embrace; it is the most comfortable position for nursing, and it happens automatically.

Babies are born expecting to have their needs met. It is the same faith that we hope to inspire in our offspring, that with hard work (and breast-feeding is very hard work for an infant—no free lunch here!) and striving, the good earth will take care of us.

But, as the old saying goes, man does not live by bread alone, and neither does the baby, before or after birth. While still inside the mother, the baby is entertained and enlivened by the symphony of the mother's body sounds and the gentle rocking of her body in motion. Some people feel there is also strong unconscious communication between the two during pregnancy. This pleasurable interaction continues after birth, since with breast-feeding the mother is totally—physically, emotionally, and spiritually—involved with the baby. It is a project for two, working together in harmony.

As pregnancy nears its completion, many mothers find small droplets of colostrum, the first milk, dried in flakes on their nipples or leaking while they lie warm and relaxed in the tub or at bedtime. The process of breastfeeding is so perfect, so natural, that it need never be interfered with. No exercises or creams, no special clothing or equipment, is needed. The colostrum is antibacterial, better than any manufactured product, and needs only to be rinsed off with clear water during the daily bath. No matter what its appearance, milky white or creamy yellow, it is fine, created for its intended consumer alone.

Couples need not be afraid to touch the breasts during lovemaking; the stimulation is good for future breastfeeding, and since colostrum is being made continuously, nothing is lost to the baby if it is tasted. Often, sexual climax will cause some of the colostrum to be ejected (this will happen during breastfeeding also, but of course in larger quantities)—a towel placed nearby can be useful if lovemaking sets off a shower of milk. The uterus will gently contract, too, caressing the baby with the reminder that this is a loving family to be part of.

For some couples it seems almost a sacrilege to "disturb" the baby with their lovemaking; they may wonder, Is sexual activity during pregnancy really safe, really part of the plan? A wise doctor once said to me, "If God had meant us to be celibate during pregnancy, he would have made women so that their vaginas shut tight at the moment of conception and not open again until the birth." Obviously, they don't; therefore, it can be safely assumed that there are reasons why sexual activity is desirable during pregnancy: the mother feels pleasure (and often relief from minor aches and pains), the father stays "pair bonded" (the old-fashioned word is "faithful"), and the baby is reminded that there are two parents!

As the physiological issues of pregnancy are resolved and the practical matters of money and making room for baby things become more settled, both members of the couple may find their thoughts turning to the emotional and spiritual issues. They may not be on the same timetable, or one may be able to deny fears and feelings more easily than the other, but eventually both will have to face their worries about the health and well-being of mother and baby during labor and delivery. The hazards of pregnancy are very real both to mother and baby. Though maternal-infant mortality and morbidity rates have fallen over the past century, there are still a very small number of pregnancies that end in tragedy: that is the reality. It is also true that adequate nutrition and the avoidance of drugs, including alcohol and cigarettes, can minimize the chance of illness or death and that many birth defects can be corrected or at least have their impact minimized.

Pregnancy, therefore, is a time of learning that total control over one's existence and its vicissitudes is unattainable, surely a lesson worth learning before attempting to raise a family. If one's life and one's children must be perfect, disappointment is inevitable. Where there is healthier respect for the vulnerability of the human condition, problems are seen in perspective, and the level of tolerance for day-to-day letdowns rises.

This time of soul-searching is a valuable part of learning to be a parent. Looking for the reasons behind fear and guilt is likely to bring up some long-buried issues that had best be resolved before the birth. Our errors and shortcomings are our teachers: we need only listen to our memories to begin spiritual housecleaning.

The issues of control over one's destiny are raised again and again during the months of pregnancy, especially in relation to the medical control of birth. While the majority of people feel that birth is a medical event and should therefore be conducted under the leadership of a professional medical team, headed by an obstetrician, there have always been some expectant parents who have questioned the authority of the physician to make life-or-death decisions. Birth, they often say, is a spiritual experience best left to the family.

The standard practice in America is for the couple to choose a health care provider, pay (or have their insurance company pay) the fee, and relinquish all responsibility to that person and/or institution. It seems plausible to feel that one has done the "right thing" by shifting the liability to the authority figure.

But buck-passing makes most thoughtful people at least a little uncomfortable, for how are they to know if they have placed their trust in someone worthy of it?

A look at the history of childbearing in the Western world is horrifying. It took the lives of many poor women before the haughty physician of the late nineteenth century deigned to disinfect his hands with chloride of lime before going from the autopsy room to the delivery room. Only a couple of generations ago, women who seemed likely to have a miscarriage were given diethylstilbestrol, a drug that was supposed to prevent the miscarriage but probably did more to cause it; not only did DES not work the wonders it was supposed to, but today many of the daughters of the women who were given it are suffering from the side effects: vaginal and uterine abnormalities, infertility and sterility, cancer-and death.

Even now, overweight women (overweight, that is, according to an official chart—as if humans were not perfect enough and needed to meet some government standards!) are indiscriminately advised to adopt low-calorie diets "to prevent complications." Of course, as in the past, many develop the complications of not following their internal calls—low birth weight babies, often with life threatening illnesses and defects.

And so, we must conclude that, although "science" may bring us technology that makes our lives easier, it may also bring useless, even harmful, intrusions into our lives. How, then, to sift the wheat from the chaff? Perhaps the best way is to measure the issue (practice, person, etc.) against the standards you hold dear by asking questions like:

Does it promote life? Humans need food; unborn babies are human; unborn babies get their food from their mothers; therefore, restricted diets in pregnancy are harmful; eating from earth's bounty is healthful.

Does it respect the sanctity of the family? The couple is the cornerstone of the family; the couple has the right to celebrate its baby's life together; therefore, to prevent husband and wife from being together at the moment their baby makes the transition from womb to world is wrong; to encourage them to work together is right.

Does it treat the whole person? A pregnant woman is more than just a physical body-within-a-body; there are spiritual and emotional connections between the pair that need to be nurtured.

Making these health decisions is part of preparing, physically, emotionally, and spiritually, for parenting, as is making decisions on the day-to-day aspects of life with a baby. The time before marriage is appropriate for sharing views on lifestyle, religion, and child rearing and for formulating a mutual philosophy. The couple can then feel their ambivalences and discuss their differences freely during the pregnancy, knowing they have their agreed-upon family philosophy to provide the guidelines they will need to establish their priorities before their baby is born.

We do not ask that our tasks be made easier;
We ask only that we be made stronger.
We do not ask that our responsibility be lighter;
We ask only that our capacity be greater.
We do not ask that our lives be perfect;
We ask only that they be graced by Your perfect love.

Welcoming

By the ninth month of pregnancy the mother's body is in full bloom. The same nutritious foods that have helped the baby attain full-term size—seven to nine pounds or more—have helped her uterus grow to thirty times its pre-pregnancy size. The muscle fibers are strong and are arranged in specifically patterned layers so that when labor starts, they will contract together in the most efficient manner, first shortening the cervix (the opening of the uterus), then pulling it up over the baby's head. Finally, when the bulk of the uterine muscle is contracted tightly at the baby's rump, it will guide first the head, then the body, through the mother's pelvic bones, through her vagina, and out into the world.

The miracle of birth is that this process happens with or without human cooperation or medical intervention. A woman's body is created to be the bearer of human young—despite what the proliferation of high-tech hospital delivery rooms and specialists may lead us to believe. Midwives and obstetricians are, at best, lifeguards, ready to act only where life and limb are threatened; at worst, they may be responsible for the very complications they then must be rescuer for.

Imagine being on a deserted island, far from "civilization," not even knowing where babies come from. Pregnancy would increase your appetite, so you would eat more of the available vegetation and, perhaps with your partner, would hunt and fish; no diet plan would be necessary, since all the available food would be nutritious. When labor approached, you would feel a natural instinct to "nest," an instinct that remains with modern day women who usually get a burst of energy for housecleaning a day or two before labor starts. (Resist those urges to superclean—it can be very tiring.) The nest would be an area sheltered from inclement weather and wild animals, perhaps with food sources nearby. Labor starts with intermittent backache or crampy feelings best relieved by walking, but when the uterine contractions increase in strength and become longer, lasting a minute or so, with only a few minutes' gap between, you would prefer to rest, perhaps leaning against a mossy bank or gently sloping tree trunk. As the intensity of each contraction grows and the baby's head is urged lower in the mother's vagina, she feels an unconstrained need to push with all her might; you would feel this need, too, whether or not you knew that it would help relieve the contractions.

Finally, the baby's head comes through the opening of the mother's vagina, stretching the tissues to their utmost. As the head passes through fully, the motion of the baby's shoulders completing the trip through the mother's pelvic bones causes the head to rotate, turning to one side. At this point you would be seeing your baby's face for the first time, reaching down in wonder at this miracle your body has been party to.

Quickly the rest of the baby slides from the mother's body, giving her relief from the intense pressure and pleasure at the sensations of separation. You would feel those sensations, not dulled by the anesthetics of modern medicine, and would be totally aware of your relationship to the child just emerged from the confines of your body.

The cold air on the baby's wet body would produce the familiar cries of discomfort that are impossible for anyone to ignore, so, drying yourself and your baby with absorbent mosses or animal skins, you would cuddle together under the watchful eye of your mate, ever ready to protect the family from marauders. Since the only comfortable way to hold a newborn is in the crook of your arm, you would find yourself in the best position for breast-feeding. (With the arm bent, the distance between the human elbow and the breast is just about the diameter of a baby's head.) Even if you knew nothing about feeding babies, in fact did not even know that there is colostrum, the earliest form of milk, present in the breast at birth, ready to protect the newborn from intestinal infections as his body acclimates to the outside world, your baby would instinctually take over, compelled by his need for what has been provided.

Babies are born with reflexes that automatically help them get nutrition. These are the rooting reflex, which causes the baby to home in on the nipple, and the sucking reflex, which removes the milk from the breast and insures that it will continue to be made in ever-increasing quantities. Your baby would likewise home in and nurse, bringing you relief from the very full feelings in your breasts and teaching you the best way to stop the wailing.

Those first cries inflate the baby's lungs, making the placenta and umbilical cord unnecessary. As the uterus begins its return to normal, the placenta is slowly peeled of the uterine wall and the umbilical cord, which was thick and pulsating with life, shrivels to the size of thin string over the next few hours. Your immediate nursing would assist this process, contracting the uterus smaller and smaller, causing the placenta to be expelled through your vagina. The hormones released by the breast-feeding stimulation would prevent you from losing a lot of blood.

The shrinking of the umbilical cord signals that there is no longer any connection between the baby's body and the placenta. Although midwives and doctors generally wait a few minutes after the birth and then clamp and cut the cord, using antiseptics to avoid infection, you would not have the tools to do this on your deserted island, nor would you think it a problem. (Hospital delivery rooms need to be cleaned up fast for the next customer, so it is unlikely their personnel would look kindly on new parents objecting to this routine procedure.) You would wait probably several hours before realizing that it might be unwieldy to carry baby and placenta, and then would most likely use whatever tool you had at hand: a flint or, more likely, your teeth. Since the blood vessels within the cord would have been closed off for hours, infection would be unlikely.

Of course, there are instances in which the natural processes need outside help to produce a healthy mother and a healthy baby; but these instances are far more rare than we have been led to believe. Occasionally, the fertilized ovum is implanted too close to the opening of the cervix, usually necessitating surgical (cesarean) delivery, and some babies end up in other that the headfirst position for birth, possibly requiring forceps or a cesarean. These "mechanical" difficulties are less frequent occurrences than one might guess from the number of cesareans performed each year. Complications are more often caused by human attempts to alter the normal course of birth.

Pain is the primary topic of concern to a great number of couples: Will it be overwhelming? What does it mean? How will we deal with it? And, above all, exactly how much pain is there? The physical perception of pain is not universal; what is excruciating to one person may be perfectly tolerable to another. In general, though, understanding the purpose and action of the uterine contraction tends to help the laboring woman perceive the pain as useful and appropriate. It is the fear of what the pain signifies that can be terrifying.

Pain is a useful sensation when it helps you identify the difference between normal functioning and a pathological situation. For most women, the pain of normal birth is tolerable; excessive pain may indicate a problem with the woman's body (such as an irregularly shaped pelvis), a problem with the spirit (such as lack of faith in one's ability), or an emotional problem (such as fear of losing their partner's attention to the new baby). Pain may also indicate an overzealous approach toward obstetrics, "active management of labor," where drugs and other interventions are used in the medical attempt to control birth. One drug in particular, oxytocin (Pitocin), causes contractions to increase in intensity and frequency in an attempt to speed the natural timetable for that birth; the lack of "time out" between contractions and their increased strength generally make some form of anesthesia or analgesia necessary. There are effects on the baby too; although no one knows if the baby perceives normal birth as painful, the increased strength and length of uterine contractions under the influence of added oxytocin often result in an increase in the fetal heart rate due to a decrease in oxygen-rich blood flowing to the placenta. (Increased heart rate is also a universal sign of fear.)

Coping with pain and stress is a learned response, one that can be mastered by the couple long before the expected birth. Taking classes that focus on relaxing and welcoming labor rather than disassociating from it strengthens the couple's ability to cope. Developing a realistic understanding of the natural process and reassuring each other of mutual faith and caring makes any physiological discomfort less frightening.

With the almost universal availability of prepared childbirth classes and books, some couples' expectations of birth have risen to the fantasy level: the mother gloriously laboring, not a hair out of place, gently comforted by her adoring husband while attended by a saintly physician leading a band of angelic nurses. When reality meets fantasy in the delivery room, the foundation for postpartum depression may be laid. It is misleading to teach that labor pain can be eradicated by merely performing some alternative activity such as rhythmic breathing or massage. The sheer power of the uterus in contraction cannot be denied.

Often the strongest advocates of prepared childbirth methods are the young fathers who gratuitously assure the young couple pregnant for the first time that birth was indeed painless, though, of course, she could not have done it without him, ever attentive to her comfort. It's best to take these stories at face value; in the effort to convince themselves that they were "successful," many couples selectively remember only the highlights. Since the best part is the moment when the baby is born, it is very easy to forget the hard work that went into reaching that point.

When plans for a natural, spiritual birth are circumvented by medical necessity, the couple may feel changed, or empowered, by the opportunity to confront their physician or midwife and get the facts straight. In most cases, there will be a demonstrable reason for medical intervention. Understanding the nature of the problem and why it was resolved the way it was is the first step to recovery and the prevention of long-term emotional pain. It is also helpful to seek out appropriate support groups, sponsored by many local childbirth and parent support groups.

Even if medical intervention is necessary, in most cases (barring true emergency situations, such as a very premature baby or very ill mother, where there will, of course, be a delay) the baby will be able to join the couple for that lovely period directly after birth known as bonding to the birth professional but just plain falling in love to the couple. Unless the couple has had very unrealistic ideas of what newborns look like (they definitely do not look like the two or three month old ones often used in movies to portray newborns!), their baby looks beautiful to them. Each little wrinkle and hair is reason for oohing and aahing; the tiny hands and feet are perfection in miniature; the eyes already looking around indicate that this baby is special. Such is the bliss of falling in love with your baby!

There has been a great rush among maternity hospitals to "humanize" the birth experience (although what could be more human than giving birth?) by dressing up their dreary, utilitarian labor rooms with curtains and hanging plants and offering optional candle-lit dinner for the new parents (usually without the baby—though nothing could be further from the reality they will soon face); the reason for such window dressing is economic. With the marked increase in the 1970s of home births and homelike, midwife-run childbearing centers, hospitals were impelled to mimic the competition or face the forced closing of their highly profitable obstetrics units. (Pediatrics units were also at risk, since most parents returned to the hospital where their baby was born for postnatal care and emergencies.) But to assume that these first moments will be somehow more loving, more perfect in a "bonding room" (or whatever title the hospital's marketing department has given what used to be called the recovery room) is no different from assuming that an exquisitely furnished church is a more reverent place to worship than a simpler refuge. The setting is unimportant; the feelings paramount.

The artistic works of the Middle Ages and early Renaissance depicted the Nativity in all its simplicity. Central in these is the Infant Jesus, the object of the adoration. Halos and auras represent the worshipful energy: He is living evidence of the worshippers' faith. So should it be with every child, for every child's birth is confirmation of the miracle of life.

Whatever the circumstances or location of the birth, there should be a private time, as soon as they are ready, for the parents to be alone to welcome, in loving adoration, their newborn. They may feel moved to pray together at the time, or they may find silence more appropriate. They may want to name their baby at this time, or perhaps sing or recite some meaningful words. Whatever they choose, their affirmation of the blessing they have received is a thank-you and amen for this personal miracle.

You are here now, little one,
Driven from your sanctuary,
Washed by the waters of that now forsaken home.
You are here now, little one,
Illumined by divine reflection of our adoration,
Blessed by our reflection of divine grace.
We do not ask who you are;
We dare not ask who you will be.
We only know that you are here
Now.

ENFOLDING

The human baby, unlike the young of most other species, is born long before even minimal self-care is possible. While calves and foals can stand on their own—if somewhat shaky—feet only hours after birth, human beings require another nine months (after the prenatal nine) before they can crawl and feed on other than their mother's milk. The reasons for this state of affairs are both biological and spiritual.

Biologically, the time of most rapid brain growth is during the last weeks of pregnancy and the first few months of life. If pregnancy were much longer than nine months, it would be impossible for the baby to get through the mother's pelvis. This rapid brain growth is accommodated by the nature of the baby's skull bones. They are not joined together, as an adult skull is, but are separate and capable of the expansion necessary to keep up with the brain as it grows. The places at which the corners of the bones come together but don't quite meet are called the fontanelles, or "soft spots," even though they are quite firm, like strong canvas. Often newborns have a pointy-headed appearance due to the pressure of vaginal birth molding the bones to fit more easily through the passageway. (Babies born surgically, missing the tight caress of birth, tend to have rounder heads at first.) Time and growth take care of these minor imperfections. But even with the mechanism of molding, the head of a baby developed enough to crawl is far too large to pass through the pelvic opening, so babies are meant to be born with this flexibility.

Spiritually, human beings are blessed with that time of total dependence as an incentive to form stable family units. Not only is the baby dependent on his parents for survival, but the new mother is dependent on her partner: she depends on him so that the baby can depend on her. Within the protection of the family, the parents learn to appreciate the individuality of each child as their uniqueness emerges, nurtured in their warmth and care. The first three months of life outside the uterus is the time of enfolding: The mother enfolds her baby literally, holding him to her breast, while the father enfolds the duo in an environment of sustenance and protection. The family needs to concentrate its collective energy on the survival of its newest member.

Many years ago, before discreet breast-feeding in public was acceptable, the uncle of a friend with a very tiny nursing baby suffered an untimely (by earthly standards) death. She felt compelled to attend the funeral but could not fathom leaving her infant behind; they would comfort each other, she reasoned. When the baby started to fret and root around for the breast, she took him to the car and sat in the back seat, peacefully nursing him. Two young cousins spied her in the car and came to investigate. Seven-year-old Debbie asked the young mother what she was doing. She replied, "I'm feeding my baby." Mystified by the apparent connection between mother and baby, eight-year-old Jon wondered, "How did you get the bottle in there?" After explaining that there was milk in her breasts as there is in every new mother, she was confronted with the next logical question. "But who gave you the milk?" Debbie inquired. She answered, "God did."

Later the young mother worried that perhaps she had misled her little cousins. After all, she reasoned, breastfeeding is a bodily function that, barring intervention, every human female is equipped to perform, not a special gift that only she was given. Their mother hadn't wanted to breast-feed, and she did not want the children to think that they had been deprived by God.

But, of course, her first response was correct. Breast-feeding is a divine gift, one that should not easily be passed up in favor of man-made substitutes. There is no perfect duplication of the product: no formula, no matter how researched and how balanced, can ever come close to duplicating a mother's milk. But even if it were possible to re-create every single nutrient, every macrophage (the living white blood cells in milk that eat up infectious invaders before they cause illness in the baby's intestines), every factor, every immunity, it would still not be a substitute for breast-feeding. The process is every bit as important as the product. In addition, the breast is the perfect container, providing cushioning softness to the baby's face while maintaining the milk at the perfect temperature and cleanliness.

Nursing a baby is economical: although the mother does need extra calories of protein, she can meet these needs with an extra glass of milk, a peanut butter sandwich on whole wheat bread, and four ounces of orange juice. Interestingly, although prices have obviously risen since 1985 when I first calculated them at less than fifty cents a day for the extra food vs. the cost of formula for one day, about two dollars, breast-feeding is still a bargain. The prices today, in 2019 are about $1.60 for the extra food vs. about $6-18 a day for the formula, depending on whether you prepare the bottles yourself, which also requires added expense for cleaning supplies and heating, plus your energy, or you buy the ready-to-go. Either way, the price of formula feeding has gone up around twice the rise in the extra nutritious food it takes to produce breast milk.

There is ecological value to breast-feeding: nothing to dispose of. There is a human ecology to breast-feeding, too, a natural ecology that preserves human resources and maximizes parental energy. This is the natural family planning effect.

Total breast-feeding—breast-feeding without supplementary formula, juice, water, or baby foods—is the natural way to space pregnancies. It means breast-feeding 'round the clock on the baby's schedule, regardless of adult preference for more feeding in the daytime hours and longer stretches of sleep at night. For many families, adopting this life-style means that they will take the baby with them wherever they go, even sleeping together in a "family bed." The constant contact between mother and baby insures frequent breast-feeding, since even during sleep the infant has access to the comfort of the breast. Total breast-feeders shun pacifiers and supplements, preferring a sort of "marsupial motherhood," like the kangaroo whose newborn stays attached to the mother's nipple until reaching the size necessary for independent food gathering.

This natural breast-feeding and the attendant flow of prolactin (often called the "mother love hormone") tend to prevent the maturation of the ovum, thus creating a temporary infertility. The nearly constant flow of prolactin, which occurs when parents are lenient about infants' sleeping hours and place, lowers the chance of conception soon after birth, which would put extra nutritional strain on the mother and would also affect the breast milk, returning it to colostrum in mid-pregnancy. It is this natural way of parenting that allows us the fullest enjoyment of each of our young.

Yet for some families, breast-feeding is difficult or impossible. In such instances, an effort can be made to duplicate many of the advantages of breast-feeding. The baby can be held in the nursing position, touching the parent's skin, and a pacifier or water bottle can be used to extend the sucking time. Above all, the spiritual quality can be experienced by reducing the amount of separation the baby must endure.

Breast-feeding is not an all-or-nothing proposition: any amount is beneficial to the family, even just feeding while in the hospital so the baby has the colostrum. But as physically and emotionally satisfying as breast-feeding is, it is not essential for good parenting. What is essential is confidence and love; guilt has no place in baby care, especially guilt over wanting (or needing) to bottle-feed.

When parenting is on the baby's schedule, feedings tend to be more frequent in the evening and early- morning hours. Perhaps this is because the fat content of breast milk tends to drop at night (lowering the caloric value and perhaps leaving the baby satisfied for a shorter period), or perhaps it is that those hours are most peaceful. With mother more relaxed, tired from the day's occupations, nursing may be more pleasurable at night than in the rush of the day. Certainly, our friends on their deserted island would find it easier to rest and nurse at night, what with daytime being the best time for food- gathering and cooking. So it may be that babies' natural inclinations to feed more frequently at night arose because of the survival value.

It is only in a wealthy society (wealthy, that is, by comparison to the rest of the world) that such "conveniences" as separate bedrooms are possible. Most of the world has no need for canopied cribs and complicated intercom systems; the mother is always with the baby. Being separated during the night seems to reduce the number of times the baby wakens to nurse; the signals that the baby gives off indicating willingness to nurse are lost, since they are unlikely to be sensed by a mother several rooms away.

While the current fashion is to 'persuade' (spelled coerce) the baby to sleep through the night as soon as possible, those whose persistence allows them to "win" are actually losers: they lose the gift of natural family spacing.

In more primitive societies babies tend to come about two or three years apart. This allows the toddler time to adjust to the regular adult diet, gradually weaning from the breast. The parents have time to recuperate from the physical strains of caring for the infant, time to renew their marital bond, time to feel the desire for another baby rather than dismay at conceiving again "too soon." The new one feels welcome even while still in the womb.

The sense of being welcomed and loved after birth continues in many ways that often have dual benefits; one of those is the sensation of being held. Everyone reaches out to hold a baby—father, grandparents, friends, and relatives of all ages vie for the opportunity for a few moments of cuddling. Being held by his parents is a baby's first sex education; the differences between male and female texture, fragrance, topography, and voice are obvious.

Although all that a baby needs can easily, and best, be satisfied by the family—food, warmth, enfolding, learning—new parents are constantly bombarded with the message that "really good parents buy our product"—whether or not, in fact, the product promotes closeness between parents and baby. More often than not, the items parents are being solicited to buy actually produce an enforced separation. Playpens, jumpers, swings, cradles, and carriages are merely places to "park" the baby so that the mother can get back to her "more important" work -cleaning, washing, and cooking. Proponents of an egalitarian life-style often decry these ads as being sexist, preferring those that show the couple together doing housework while the baby sits alone in a walker. But neither way is as graceful as showing the father vacuuming the carpet while the mother sits contentedly performing the task that only she can do: breastfeeding!

Most men realize soon after the birth that things are not likely to return to normal for a very long time, especially in the area of housekeeping. Those men who have been used to their wives handling virtually all the cooking, cleaning, and laundry may be in for a rude shock! These seemingly simple tasks take an incredibly large amount of time, and since the mother of a newborn has that baby's care and feeding as her top priority and since she can't possibly be in two places at once, many chores will be left undone.

There are some very practical things that a new father can do to keep the household running and the new family functioning. One extremely useful thing is just not add to the clutter. If yours has not been a particularly organized household, even a few cartons or laundry baskets can help control the "visual pollution" and give an overall impression of tidiness; they can also prevent the loss of important papers or objects by providing an instant sorting center for those items that need to be dealt with later.

If part-time household help is financially feasible, it can be of tremendous practical and emotional help to the whole family. Mother can gain confidence in caring for the new infant, and her partner can return to a household where she is not overly stressed and where the house itself is in order.

The most important thing is to keep the mother and baby loved and comfortable, so make sure that both of them are supplied with the food and clothing they need. However, as long as there is something nutritious on the table, it doesn't really matter if it's a gourmet banquet on fine china or hamburgers and salad served up on paper plates. What counts is the caring, and this is best done in a simple way. This is also true for the laundry: as long as there are clean clothes in the closet and clean towels in the bathroom, the household can run smoothly. The new mother will ease back into managing the home as her confidence and strength grow, but in the interim it's good if she understands that her partner has things under control without her having to ask.

The real shame of the forces that act against the baby's need to be held and nurtured is that they also damage the mother in that they interfere with her need for retreat during the first few months after birth. Although physiologically oriented textbooks give six weeks as the recovery period for childbirth, most women require twice that time before they feel ready to fully resume their pre-pregnant lives, including household and community responsibilities. By offering her substitutes for what are really the pleasures—holding and feeding the baby—she may be hearing that her real worth is as a consumer of goods and services, and the sooner she gets back to earning (at a job that is may be less rewarding, in all ways, than caring for her baby) and spending (for things she and her baby neither need nor want) the happier she'll be. It seems absurd to have new mothers rush back to work only to spend the additional dollars on substitutes for her milk, her arms, her very presence, but that is very much the state of things in any society that devalues the family.

Women are not the only victims in a society that gives out confused messages about the desirability of being a parent; fathers, too, suffer a bewilderment of conflicting advice about what their role should be. But to accept merely a role—a function, a part—rather than be fully yourself, in parenting as well as in the rest of your life, is to live two-dimensionally. Being a parent requires more than following someone else's set of dos and don'ts.

Rather than attempt to fulfill the narrowly-rimmed, ancient job descriptions for Mother and Father, both parents need to concentrate on being their most intimate and trusting selves with each other and their baby, for it is intimacy and trust that are the first gifts passed from parents to child. Where intimacy and trust are actively pursued, there is no room for rejection and despair. Where there is faith and devotion, no father feels like a meal ticket and no mother describes herself as "just a mother."

Rather than try to force parents and babies into some

artificial mode of interacting, we need to rediscover the nearly lost art of natural parenting. Where life's progression is allowed to flow undammed, no infant grows into an insecure, self-abnegating child. Where the spontaneous response to need is love, no family is fragmented.

Enfolded in Your lightness,
We learn to enfold our child in our lightness.
Drawing strength and sustenance from us,
Our child teaches us to draw strength and sustenance
From You.
We are the medium through which Life flows
Between our Creator and our
Creation.

Unfolding

The need for a loving, trusting relationship between parents and baby intensifies as the baby's struggle toward autonomy begins. Becoming a person in your own right can be difficult, but where all family members have feelings of trust in and commitment to one another, parents feel secure in their abilities to shepherd their children through the early years. Under these conditions babies maintain an uninterrupted, unrestrained curiosity about their surroundings and sustain their natural instinct to master the social, motor, communication, and creative skills needed to satisfy and heighten that curiosity.

The baby's third-month birthday actually marks the end of the first year of parenting (nine months before birth plus three after) and the end of the very intense period of total enfolding. By this anniversary faith has matured into confidence and the family is ready to unfold and begin the very gentle nudging toward maturity that for the next eighteen or so years will comprise their most important task as parents.

The most startling changes taking place at this time are in the area of mobility. One morning you waken to find the baby you were positive was sleeping peacefully on his tummy, now gurgling with joy on his back, arms and legs dancing wildly in the air. Not so long afterward, the chubby little legs that once seemed so fragile are efficiently propelling their owner across the room, now requiring a safe area under a parent's watchful eye.

No special training or exercise program is necessary for the development of these skills: it is children's nature to push themselves to the limit. It is only indirectly (in the absence of disease) that a baby's drive to move can be adversely affected; this might occur if the loving attention needed to maintain sufficient feelings of trust and curiosity is distant or denied.

This attention needs to come from both parents. It is more than just taking care of the baby's needs for feeding and diapering; it includes singing and talking, exercising and playing, and introducing the world's wonders and mysteries.

Somewhere around the third month most babies will have learned to turn from back to front and back over again, by using their neck, shoulder, arm, and hand muscles. The age at which this accomplishment takes place is not a predictor of future intelligence but seems to be more connected to the infant's unique style. Babies that are always in motion, nap infrequently, and fuss more than average seem to discover (sometimes totally serendipitously!) how to roll over faster than the more placid, peaceful ones.

First-time parents, especially those who have not spent much time with babies, are often intimidated by textbook timetables and by parents who brag of their infant's accomplishments. One loving grandfather tells a story that is even more absurd than the usual "my kid's smarter than yours" tale. It seems that shortly after the birth of grandchild number one, grandfather found himself in his dentist's chair, swapping stories with the dentist, who had also just recently become the grandfather of a healthy little boy. He chanced to remark that his grandson, at the ripe old age of five months, already had his first tooth. The dentist, perhaps feeling beaten at his own game, had to admit that his grandson, six-and-a-half months old, had yet to cut his first incisor. However, he averred, reaching for his drill, "the later the teeth, the longer you keep them."

The story is repeated here not to suggest that late teethers have healthier teeth (not true, but neither do earlier teethers—the healthiest teeth belong to those who brush, floss, eat well, and see their dentist and dental hygienist twice a year) but to illustrate the lengths to which some people will go to prove to themselves that they are good enough parents or grandparents.

Along the same line, many parents claim to have babies who sleep through the night when what they really have are babies who don't fuss too much and go back to sleep before either parent wakens to investigate. Unfortunately, all this serious competition does is make parents who are honest with themselves and admit to their human failings occasionally suspect that something is very wrong with their perfectly normal family.

Doctors are often victims of this subterfuge too. If all their patients' parents affirm that their child sleeps through the night and wakens only once every four hours, as if gifted with an internal clock, how can they help but believe that all babies should be like that and to deviate from that norm may spell disaster?

The fact is that schedules and timetables are based on averages, and average does not mean the same as normal. There is no comparison standard for your baby, no quality control guidelines for your family. There is only respecting each individual and their efforts to master the tasks of living.

Around the same time that rolling and head-holding are mastered, most babies begin to make random sounds in a kind of primitive communication. This is the time when responding to the cooing and gurgling is apt to earn you a happy, toothless grin. Responding doesn't have to be limited to baby talk: babies love to hear about your day, your plans, local politics, or whatever. They talk back, struggling to imitate your mouth movements, and are wonderful mimics of cadence and melody. By talking to your baby, you reinforce the sounds that your baby will need to master your language, no matter what that language is. (That is why people who immigrate in adulthood retain the accents of their childhood and may never be able to master some of the phonemes peculiar to their adopted country.)

There is an old story about a very wealthy and very curious man who wanted to know what language babies would learn to speak if they never heard any sounds. He constructed a fantastic nursery, with cradles and toys and nurses to care for the infants. (I do not know where he got the infants from, but this is a legend, so let us assume that they just appeared in their cradles.) The nurses were instructed to feed and dress their charges but were forbidden to talk to them. Nursery rhymes, pat-a-cake games, songs, and even humming were banned, all in the effort to learn which of the earth's many languages was the true language of man.

The experiment, as you may have guessed, was a failure: all the babies died. Deprived of their parents' chatter and play, they became apathetic and lost their desire for human contact, much as a depressed adult withdraws from life, denying his spirit.

This is just a story, and an old one at that, but parents are still being told (mercifully less often and less forcefully) not to "spoil" their babies with "too much" contact. This is nonsense, as any sensitive parent understands: you cannot spoil a baby with love. The classic "spoiled" child is the one who demands things, who has no sense of the value of human relationships. This "spoiling" is easily accomplished by just substituting an object—new toy, sweet snack, paid entertainer (human or electronic)—for yourself, your time, your attention. For your baby only the best will do, and the best is you.

Eventually all that time and attention pays off, and somewhere around the time a baby learns to navigate safely, holding on to furniture or a reassuring adult hand, the first recognizable word is heard. Recognizable to a parent, that is, but not necessarily understood as being any different from his usual babbling to the baby. It is the reinforcement, the repeating of the word back to the baby, that makes it a meaningful addition to his growing vocabulary.

At around the seventh month or so, most babies' neuromuscular development is advanced enough to allow for sitting without being propped up. This is a good time for the baby to sit at the dinner table either in a high chair or securely harnessed to a booster seat. The baby's sociability is developing and he is ready to learn good table manners by imitation, of course. At the same time, the fine motor skills have advanced from just reaching for and grabbing objects (especially glasses and dangling earrings) to being able to propel the object neatly into his mouth. These skills mature at the same time that teething starts, altogether quite the sensible time to add solid foods to the baby's diet.

The advantages to waiting to diversify the diet until this time are many, not the least important of which is that feeding your baby from those tiny (but expensive) jars of strained mush is tedious, time-consuming, and terribly messy for you, your baby, and the immediate environment.

Not so long ago, before pediatricians got together and finally declared that babies do not need solid food before the middle of the first year, variety of diet was a competitive issue in some social circles. It seems absurd now, but the theory seemed to be that if the pediatrician said you could give your baby strained avocado or mashed rutabaga, your child must be advanced far beyond the child next door, whose pediatrician limited solid food to an occasional sliver of banana. These issues probably go through cycles: in the nineteen twenties and thirties the issue was how well your baby kept to the prescribed feeding/sleeping schedule; the nineteen forties and fifties parent concentrated on speedy toilet training; the sixties and seventies seemed to concentrate on solid food; the major competitive area of the eighties was vocabulary; and in the nineties home computers became ubiquitous, along with videos aimed at babies well below Sesame Street age. I began to wonder around the turn of this century if babies in this millennium would have their own social networking site interfacing with their parents' while still in the womb.

While not harmful to babies in and of itself, the parenting Olympics does nothing to help focus on the uniqueness of every child. In this respect, such competitiveness obscures the graceful feelings and contributes to parental dissatisfaction; dissatisfied people seek to blame someone or something for their feelings. Whether they blame the child for his (real or imagined) shortcomings or themselves for being less-than-perfect parents, the result is the same: guilt and alienation, often leading to despair.

A task of the baby's first year, as important as preparing to walk and talk, is learning that he is a separate, distinct individual. More than just satisfaction of the drive toward independent action, this process of becoming a singular person is a complete transformation from the total at-oneness of pregnancy and the first three months outside, to a human being, wholly different from either parent.

This movement toward self-containment is easier for the

baby who is blessed with parents who have themselves been able to feel a strong sense of self. Parents who have a "scrambled eggs" relationship with their own parents are still fighting for their own identity; this makes their baby's task harder.

But becoming a parent can be a healing experience for those whose transition from womb to world was not buffered by an intense enfolded period. They can come to a mature, conscious understanding that their parents also missed the developmental stage of parenting that is necessary to be able to let go of the child, to gradually encourage the sense of autonomy. They can put forth the needed effort to experience fully the giving of birth and sustenance to their little one, retaining the perspective of the adult member of the parent-infant dyad, even though they feel strong needs to be parented themselves. While in this intense time of their baby's need for them, they may want to find another source for the parenting they missed but now so sorely desire. Ideally, the couple can do this for each other, recognizing that this phase of constant dependence will soon end.

Thus nourished by each other, both parents can more clearly identify and respect their baby's attempts toward autonomy and support them without fearing that they are being either too protective or too presumptuous.

A safe guideline for knowing when to encourage independence and when to offer unconditional sanctuary to the toddler is to err on the side of sanctuary, offering it but not demanding it be taken, especially when the child is tired, cranky, or crying.

Common sense goes a long way when dealing with babies: their crying is annoying precisely because that's the best way for them to get your attention. Their drive is to communicate that they need you, not that they want to make you feel uncomfortable. Their need for you does not stop just because the clock says bedtime.

There is an old saying, "If your little children are not allowed to disturb your sleep in little ways, then surely, when they are big, they will disturb your sleep in big ways." And so it is, that if a child's needs are not met in the right season, they will not evaporate but will grow stronger in the next one.

*Let our hearts acknowledge
The futility of trying
To hold summer's sunlight,
To stall autumn's harvest,
To trap winter's windsong,
To save springtime's blossom;
Enjoin us from heeding
Any hourglass save Your own
For this child,
Your masterwork.*

WORKING

This country, it would appear, is more pro-business than pro-family: there are no federal standards or guidelines for maternity leave other than the proviso that childbirth and parenthood be treated as any other disease, chargeable against any sick leave accrued by the "victim," and an affliction to recover from in due course. (To those who find it difficult to believe that the government "experts" would equate a natural process with a disease, it can only be pointed out that these are often the same people who equate the fetus with a tumorous mass of tissue.)

Perhaps, buried under the equal opportunity rules and regulations, there is still some pro-parenthood sentiment; if so, it is increasingly difficult to find, as inflation, bureaucratic growth, and heavy taxation place additional burdens on the one-wage-earner family, forcing many women to enter or remain in the work force despite their desire to provide their children with the best possible upbringing.

For other women, working vs. mothering is more than just an issue of economics: they (and research backs them up) believe that to interrupt the course of their employment would spell the end of advancement. Even though motherhood is itself an educational experience that develops many of the character traits so valuable to potential employers, women—and especially their potential employers—are still being duped by the popular notion that mothering is mindless.

Certainly, if zero population growth is to be a national goal, discouraging women from discovering the pleasures of motherhood would tend to keep them out of the home and in the workplace. The result of these mixed messages about working and mothering is a great deal of confusion and guilt for those women who want to raise children and want to—or must—work.

Less than a century ago, and even today in many parts of the world, working and mothering was not an issue. Home-based industries like farming and family-owned stores meant the entire family worked together for their mutual good: children were assigned tasks that contributed to the family's well-being to the level of their ability, and mother, being an essential part of management, didn't have to ask if she could have maternity leave or an on-premises day-care center. She might be nursing the newest family member while balancing the books or ordering seed, but she could fulfill her family's economic and emotional needs at the same time, and probably had precious few moments to think about her dual role.

In the post-Second World War years, the "baby boom," the false sense of economic security sent many women happily home from the factories: the new idea of "togetherness" was not about the social- economic togetherness of the family farm but was rather mother (the at-home parent) and father (the at-work parent) gathering around the barbecue with the kids for a pallid imitation of the mutuality inherent where survival was the primary goal of the family.

Today the issue is still "quality time," the theory being that it is better to spend fewer hours with your child as long as these are intense, meaningful hours. The flaw in the theory is that prime time is always when the parent has a bare spot in the schedule, not when the child's need for the parent is most intense. And, as studies show, the actual amount of contact time in these situations is usually far less than the parent believes and far less than the child requires for emotional and spiritual development.

Actually, what children of working and nonworking mothers alike need is "nonquality time"—those moments filled with the sheer pleasure of doing nothing together. It is the spontaneous, unplanned time—just being together and experiencing together—that is often the most satisfying and memorable part of the child's growing up.

Unfortunately, in all the debates and studies the one voice that is consistently disregarded is that of the one person who is affected most by the issue: the child. It is the child who needs the mother most, the child who feels her absence most acutely. Psychologists tell us that by the end of the first year most children have developed "object permanency"—the understanding that when an object is hidden from sight it continues to exist. Therefore, the child can tolerate the mother's absence. But it is difficult to believe that this permanency is the same for a ball that rolls under a couch and the mother, whose very existence is essential to the child's well-being.

It is not the mother's paid employment that is unhealthy for the child, but rather, her absence for long periods of time. Indeed, some women, feeling that mothers should not work yet not objecting to paying someone to care for the baby, fill their hours with volunteering, clubs, and the like. The result may be less time with the baby than the mother who works for financial reasons and rushes home, eager to enjoy every moment with her family.

Some mothers try working at home (admittedly easier for us writer-mothers), fitting their time at the computer or sewing machine into the naptimes and odd half-hours when the baby is busy entertaining other family members. Like all compromises, working at home is less than perfect for all concerned: the mother can feel very rushed and overburdened as deadlines loom, while the baby may not always get the mother's undivided attention. Still, it is one imperfect way to deal with the conflict between the very different needs of mother and child. (One advantage, not often considered, is that working at home cuts down on the expense of a business wardrobe, lunches out, and transportation, so one can net the same dollar amount in a shorter period.)

A less effective but no less popular practice is to return to work as soon after giving birth as physically possible, for economic, career, or both reasons, secretly enjoying the busy life but crying *mea culpa* to anyone willing to help assuage the guilt. But this kind of guilt is self-indulgent: it serves no useful end but rather asks for forgiveness where none is needed.

Mothers who must (out of economic or personal necessity) return to work while their babies are still quite young can maximize the time they have for mothering by continuing to nurse even after returning to work. The easiest way to accomplish the continuation of breastfeeding is to nurse more frequently at night, nurse before leaving for work, and express milk into a container at lunchtime. By encouraging nursing and playtime in the late evening and early morning, many working mothers have found that they can actually reverse their baby's night and day, at least during infancy.

Working mothers also need to learn to delegate housework or learn to live in a less-than-perfect environment. The combined commitments to baby and job leave little enough room for unscheduled time: to waste those precious moments on things instead of people is senseless. They also need to beg off volunteer work for the duration and remember that charity begins at home.

For many women the issue is not whether to return to work, but when. Some say as soon after the birth as possible, to minimize the mother's sense of loss (since presumably she would have not grown very close to the baby in a short period of time): what they are really saying is that the less involvement, the less pain. Yet these people would be shocked if it were suggested to them to live apart from their spouses to minimize the impact of death or divorce.

To love a baby—to feel deeply and passionately about the baby's well-being—intensifies both the pleasures and the pains, just as with any other love relationship.

There is no magic time, no special age at which a baby (and mother) feels the separation less acutely. As more and more fathers are involved in the births and early moments of their children's lives, they, too, feel the absence during their workday: passionate parenting is not limited to women.

How, then, to reconcile the needs of mother, father, baby, family? No universal pattern fits all equally; no parceling out of hours and half-hours is as satisfactory as spontaneity. Each family must consider what the individual and group needs are, and how they can be met within the family. For instance, work outside the home may be attractive primarily because it satisfies the mother's need for socializing with other productive adults:

if so, she may consider becoming active in volunteer work where babies are welcome adjutants. The mother whose primary motivation is money may find alternative work that is compatible with her baby's need to be with her.

Some couples try working different shifts so that the baby care is shared and parent substitutes are unnecessary. While this arrangement may be acceptable to the baby, in the long run it becomes wearing on the parents, who miss the time they had together before the birth of their child.

Today many husbands are taking "paternity leaves" from their jobs and are remaining home for anywhere from a few days to a few months in order to take the opportunity to witness and enjoy their child's first weeks and months of life. In many cases this allows the mother to return to her job earlier than she might otherwise, if, in fact, she has chosen to return to work.

The "house-husband" phenomenon is clearly gaining in popularity as men find that there is nothing wrong with staying home while their children are young. In fact, the experience is often one of the most rewarding of their lives.

Parenthood is a calling: one we answer to every moment of our children's lives. Embracing that calling, we agree to fulfill the "job description," to care for the souls entrusted to us, to prepare them for maturity, to guide and enlighten, to inspire and be inspired.

The work you have given us
Fills our lives with purpose
And sweetens us with achievement.
Help us weave our obligations
Into the perfect pattern of
The goal You have for us.

Playing

No parent needs to be taught how to play with an infant: the universal game is getting a baby to smile and coo. But for toddlers, play is a more serious proposition. It is their work, their way of learning how to navigate in society through their interactions with others, and their mode of developing mastery over their environment.

Children's play is practice and preparation for life: this is why preschoolers and kindergarteners love to dress in grownups' clothing and play house. Any mother who has heard her daughter talking to her dolls knows how well children learn to imitate the nuances of voice tone and gestures of their family role models. While imitating the peculiarities of their parents, children absorb their unspoken standards and ethics. This is why play is such a strong medium for the transmission of family values.

The old dictum "Do what I say, not what I do" doesn't work with small children. They understand the concepts of good and bad by the third birthday and need to believe in the consistent goodness of their parents. Therefore, they strive to imitate even the less desirable behaviors rather than accept that their parents might be less than perfect and have higher expectations and aspirations for their offspring than they do for themselves. Although this may make life with children uncomfortable at times, it does serve to motivate parents to think through the reasons for the disparity in their values and actions and to work toward greater harmony in their own lives.

Children don't think of play as something separate from the other tasks of life. It is only relatively recently that elaborate educational toys designed to provide developmentally appropriate experiences have been available: formerly, children's playthings consisted of household castoffs such as an old pot and a wooden spoon, empty thread spools and thick twine for stringing, and old newspapers and magazines for tearing and scribbling on. Although the new toys are pretty, nontoxic, and educator—approved, they seem complete unto themselves, less likely to involve the imagination and less likely to require parental involvement.

A good example is the doll, which has evolved from a rough imitation of a baby to an elaborately dressed and equipped duplicate. The simple rag doll did not demand a package of tiny disposable diapers from the toy store. It did inspire problem-solving, not unlike the first woman wrapping an animal skin around her baby's bottom to keep herself (and baby) dry, and it provided an excellent introduction to the motherly art of making something that will work from the scraps you have saved. It transmitted the family ethic of providing for the young in a very direct way. In contrast, the modern doll whose wardrobe matches the child's in both quantity and quality leaves little room for imagination and mutual problem solving between parent and child.

Likewise, storytelling can be either a spirited encounter between parent and child or a boring, joyless duty. Children do like to hear their favorite stories over and over again, often to the distress of parents, especially when the frequently requested stories are of the highly commercial, "age-graded" sort, with few words and even less meaning. For many children, asking to have a book read over and over seems more like a plea to keep the parent talking and paying attention to the child than a way of mastering a developmental task.

Old-fashioned spontaneous storytelling is the best way to circumvent the prepackaged quality of many children's books. One doesn't need the imagination of a novelist to be a storyteller: stories are all around and we merely have to look for them. The Bible is, of course, a perfect reference, while collections of fairy tales, folktales, and fables can provide themes for stories. Each tale can then be put into words that the child will understand, and any undesired parts, such as violence, can be edited out. As the child grows older, the classic stories grow with him until he is old enough to appreciate reading the originals alone.

Prescreening the books your child has access to is a parental duty, not so much for censorship (for what is censored becomes more attractive) but to bring up in conversation those points you agree or disagree with. For instance, a very popular series of books aimed at preschoolers features a cat whose mischievous behavior with two small children takes place after their mother has left them alone in the house. Although the books are funny and probably do contribute to learning to read, since children respond to the repetitive rhymes, the stories may be frightening to a sensitive child who asks himself, "What would I do if my parents left me alone and a strange creature came to the door?"

It's not enough just to prescreen for negative issues. Seeking out books, television programs, and community events that are positive reinforcements for the values you would like your children to have is also a parental responsibility.

The issue of what religion the child will be brought up in should, of course, have been settled before his conception; still, many parents never consider the issue, believing that they will send the child to a Sunday school at the proper age and leave the matter to professionals. This sort of religious education generally starts at the same time as the child's secular education, bypassing the most important time for acquainting children with God.

Toddlerhood is a wonderful time for rituals and celebrations, especially those that happen on a regular basis. Toddlers need help defining the limits of acceptable and desirable behavior; invoking a greater benevolent authority than their parents helps children develop their spiritual perspective of themselves.

Saying prayers at bedtime is a ritual that toddlers enjoy. Praying with your child can start even before the child is old enough to understand what is being said; the hushed moments before the devotion is said can be used to focus on the child, asking God's blessing for him. Later, when toddlers understand the reason why the prayers are said, they may spontaneously add their own in a very natural expression of their own spiritual side.

Saying grace before meals starts out as a sort of game to a toddler: the rules are that we first are very quiet, then one person recites and the others acknowledge with an amen, and only then do we eat. Since every family member participates in this ritual, it is not just a rule for children (like no talking while mother and father are discussing important business) but a special moment at which all are equal in the eyes of God. When a child is four or five, he should be encouraged to participate by saying his own simple prayer. Saying thank you for the simplest meal before and after dining makes it all the more natural for a child to say please and thank you, not meaninglessly, but as an acknowledgment of the dignity and importance of other people.

Holidays are special times for the whole family: the traditions that are handed down from each parent's family are blended, giving visible evidence of the bonding that has taken place between the father and the mother. When the children are small and time and energy are at a premium, some of the most labor-intensive customs may have to be modified or put aside in order to truly celebrate the holiday. Christmas, for instance, which should be a joyous, spiritual celebration of peace on earth, has deteriorated into a frantic race of decorating, cooking, and gift-buying, exhausting everyone, especially the toddler, who gets left with a baby-sitter or pushed along through crowded, noisy stores, never able to understand the purpose behind the rush.

There is a great drive to make the baby's first Christmas a memorable one, with gifts piled high and numerous videos detailing the day's events. In future years the child will have two sets of memories: the day as depicted in the pictures, and the memories of the feelings associated with the holiday. Of the two, the feeling memories are most important, encapsulating as they do his feelings about himself and his family. Therefore, it is more important to respect the little one's needs at these times than to have the kind of elegant celebration that is possible when there are no children. There will be fewer Christmas cookies when toddlers' little fingers have shaped the dough, but they will be baked with loving feelings. There may not be money available for an ornate Christmas tree sparkling with breakable glass ornaments and hazardous candles, but there can be the shared value of caring for the birds by wreathing an outdoor tree with garlands of popcorn and caring for the less fortunate by giving away items the family no longer needs. For despite the commercialism and tales of Santa Claus, with his elves and reindeer, Christmas is, after all, the celebration of the birth of Christ. While children may not understand the religious significance immediately, they do understand that birthdays are to be celebrated; some families with toddlers have a birthday cake and sing, "Happy Birthday, dear Jesus."

In order to familiarize the child with the story of Jesus' birth, the family might read the passages in the Gospel of Luke that recount the episode. Several simplified translations are available, which are more easily understood by young children, or you may just recount the story in your own words—always the most engaging way to delight your child.

Sharing is thus learned as a ritual long before a child is capable of understanding that it is more blessed to give than to receive. Taught by example, in the context of family tradition, sharing life's blessings becomes a natural act: it is pleasurable to share because we are rewarded for it, first with our parents' delight in us, then with our realization that sharing is an act reflecting God's grace. Passing this ritual of sharing on to our children provides them with the most important social skill for cooperative play.

Rituals are also a child's way of mastering the environment. With a parent's help, even a very young child can learn to keep toys and clothing in order. By providing the framework—low shelves, bins, drawers—parents help their child learn to categorize and sort things. By repeating the ritual at the end of the day, concepts of same and different become part of the child's thinking process in a natural way.

Being successful at controlling the orderliness of his possessions reinforces the lessons and increases the child's self-esteem—with the added benefit of less work for parents!

This type of practical learning is valuable to the entire family because it has real purpose. In contrast, there is a kind of learning through play that by its close resemblance to performing animals' tricks, seems somehow dehumanizing to the child. This is the rote learning of letters, numbers, and the like from television programs aimed at preschoolers. These shows have been praised and awarded so much for their assumed contributions to learning that there has been little room for criticism of the one-sided sort of teaching.

Rather than reward social interaction, this sort of training rewards only performance, whether it has value at the time or not. Admittedly, it is amusing to hear a two-year-old recite the alphabet and count to twenty, but it seems more like listening to a parrot, less like the joy of knowing that your child understands the meaning of words and symbols.

There is probably no harm in allowing small children to watch very limited amounts of educational television, but the warning needs to be stated that watching one program usually leads to watching another, and so on, until the television becomes the total electronic babysitter and the special benefits of direct parent-child interaction are lost.

Standard children's programming, while for the most part not harmful, may require parental interpretation to reinforce the good parts and play down the bad. This requires that parents actually watch the shows so that the difference between real (the news, for instance) and the make-believe (cartoons and fairy tales) can be emphasized, although most children cannot spontaneously distinguish the difference before age six. Commercials provide a vehicle for helping the child become an informed consumer, especially if parents share their reasons for refusing to be influenced to purchase overpriced, heavily advertised toys.

By the same token, the good parts, which show tender, loving relationships, caring for the less fortunate, and other ethics you wish to promote, can be enjoyed together, teaching by example the appreciation of value.

Teaching the appreciation of value in all areas of life is done first by example, and later by presenting limited choices to your child. This can be done with food by offering a choice of various good foods rather than a choice between good and junk food. With television, the choices could include a few suitable programs and some alternatives, such as a half-hour of playing catch or reading a favorite book together.

There are physical effects when television is relied on for entertainment, the most obvious of which is that the more television, the less physical activity the child has time for. The television stays in one place no matter how active the program's actors appear to be; whatever learning there is, is like a lecture. In contrast, active teaching happens spontaneously when a parent is active with a child. There is constant change, the involvement of mind, body, and spirit.

Another drawback of television is that children can do it alone, yet they are not really alone with their own thoughts. They miss the opportunity to enjoy solitary activity and enhance their imagination and creativity. At the same time, they may watch television with others, giving them the illusion of cooperative play, but they don't really socialize. Of the different modes of play-alone, with a parent, with agemates, with a machine—television, and now computer, seems the least likely to meet the true goals of play.

Play is for feeling and learning, for exercising and socializing, but mainly it is for fun. Becoming proficient at playing is a lifelong project begun in infancy and, for too many people, cut off prematurely, interrupting the free flow of the natural expression of vitality and joy.

Lord, help us to keep the balance
Of work and play and prayer;
And help us to remember how we were as children:
So intent, so absorbed in our daily labors,
That all in the same moment
We worked and played and prayed.

Disciplining

The time between the child's second and third birthdays is called by many weary parents "the terrible twos." The charming antics of the young toddler exploring his environment and learning to walk and communicate seem to change overnight into willful, mischievous disobedience. So frustrating is the normal behavior of the two-year-old that even the most relaxed parents may find themselves at wit's end, trying to figure out how to bend—if not break—their child's will. Recalling their own childhoods, they may have conflicts about the way they were disciplined, especially if their parents used the old (and not very effective) "put the fear of God in them" method, and they have finally come to love, not fear, God in their adulthood.

The much-quoted "spare the rod and spoil the child" has historically been used to justify physical punishment of even very young children in the effort to prevent demanding behavior, yet viewed within the context of the Twenty-third Psalm, this seems as absurd as trying to equate love and fear.

The Psalm opens, "The Lord is my shepherd"; the metaphors that follow describe the relationship of man to his Creator as that of the lamb to his guardian. The shepherd neither deprives nor overindulges his charges but brings them to the grazing fields, where they are allowed to satisfy their innate needs. No lamb is coerced into perpetual infancy or prematurely advanced to the status of full-grown ewe or ram. No infant lamb is "spoiled" by the tender ministrations of the shepherd, because he knows that this need for extra care will not extend interminably.

The Psalm goes on to describe how the Lord's flock need fear no harm while in His care: "Yea, though I walk through the valley of the shadow of death, I will fear no evil, for Thou art with me; Thy rod and Thy staff, they comfort me." No rod of punishment is described here, but only the power of loving guidance used in concert with the staff of support and sustenance. This is the discipline that inspires growth of body, mind, and spirit in the young child.

Like little lambs, children need to learn to move with the flock. For the two- or three-year-old, the tasks of socialization include weaning, toilet training, putting himself to sleep, and learning to wash, dress, and perform basic tasks of grooming. Paradoxically, sometimes our children's biggest barrier to accomplishing these tasks is what we, their parents, hold in our minds. If we believe our children are unwilling to go to bed at a reasonable hour, most likely they will still be awake when we are ready to go to sleep.

On the other hand, what we believe about their abilities can motivate them to live up to our expectations.

These early tasks are complicated by the child's perception of the world. So much less sophisticated than adults, children constantly need reassurance that we will be their shepherds, protecting them from harm, even when that harm is an illusion. For example, two year olds have no sense of relative size, so the fear they have of falling into the toilet or being sucked into the bathtub drain with the waste water is realistic within their understanding of the way the physical world operates.

Likewise, children vary in their ability to wean themselves from the breast or bottle to the cup, depending on how they view the availability of substitutes: if the breast or bottle was also their comforter, it will be more difficult to give up, while the child with a different object for self-pacifying—an old blanket or teddy bear, for instance, may find the transition less traumatic. If weaning occurs gradually and the child is allowed some indulgence at the particularly difficult points—the birth of another baby or the mother's return to the work force, for example, growing up will feel more a privilege than deprivation.

The goal of parental discipline should be the achievement of the child's self-discipline, not parental control of the child's behavior. There is a rational basis for moral behavior—the

Golden Rule, "Do unto others as you would have them do unto you," is a universal standard, appearing in some form in all the world's cultures and religions. Disciplining in a rational manner, with the objective of increasing self-control, relies on the child's desire to emulate those he loves, not on fear of the consequences of misbehavior. To rule by fear means that the goal is not self-control, which develops in an atmosphere of love and trust, but that the desired result is blind obedience to authority. Love and trust build faith, whether that is the faith a child has that his parents will always care for him or the faith that a loving Creator who allows us the freedom to stumble and fall engenders in the devoutly religious.

This is not to say that a disciplined child will simply arise from the parents' love. Even the calmest person can succumb to the frustration of the third glass of milk spilled at the same meal and end up shrieking and threatening mayhem. If you find yourself flying off the handle at relatively minor things, perhaps the change needs to come from within yourself rather than from your child.

If stress levels within the family are high and unavoidable (due, perhaps, to sudden loss of employment or severe illness of a family member) using positive means of coping, such as prayer, meditation, or seeking counseling, is a way to demonstrate effective modes of dealing with the crises—large and small—of life.

Parents need to understand what can realistically be expected from their child at every age so they can set attainable standards. These are the standards that are set at the level at which your child will experience success most of the time. For example, it would be unrealistic to expect a three-year-old to keep his room perfectly neat, but a child of that age could certainly put all the blocks on the shelf or put all the socks in the right drawer. Standards can be raised as the child matures, so there is always a bit of challenge, yet successful performance remains likely. With steady, gentle reminders, most children will learn to help with chores, rewarded by the sense of accomplishment for their achievements. As long as there is praise for a job well done (a simple thank you, no gushing) and no undue criticism for less-than-ideal behavior, the emphasis will remain on the child's accomplishment, encouraging self-esteem.

Whenever possible, it's best to avoid the terms good and bad when applied to the child. No child is all one or the other; it is especially confusing when the terms are used to evaluate behavior in relation to what the parent would like the child to do. If obeying the parent is always praised as good and disobeying (or failing a task) is always bad, the child does not learn to differentiate between his feelings and his parents' feelings. This separation is a vital part of becoming a mature individual: it starts early in life in small ways and continues through to early adulthood.

Children have literal minds: they take you at your word. If that word is always thoughtful and loving, your child develops trust in his world. But if you lose your temper repeatedly and threaten your child with bodily harm, abandonment, or divine retribution, your child will feel that the world is a threatening place and may feel the need to fight back in even more antisocial ways. Ridicule and shame likewise have no place in discipline, tending as they do to produce guilt rather than the desire to cooperate.

Discipline is like the stick a tree farmer ties to a young seedling: it is a guide to growing straight that is held firm to the very small sprout and is loosened as the fledgling tree grows. Guiding a child means very close observation is needed until the self-control is well in evidence; until then parents need to be aware of temptations that may be impossible for the child to resist. Childproofing a home is difficult: there are a thousand temptations for a child to explore that adults don't see, including electrical sockets, matches and lighters, pills ("Childproof" containers are something of a misnomer. Most children find them easier to open than adults do!), and anything small enough to be swallowed or poked up a nose or in an ear. In the early years safety and discipline are firmly intertwined.

During the (not always) terrible twos, children often feel frustrated when they are unable to accomplish what they want to, especially if there are older siblings or neighbors with whom the toddler wants to play. The result of this sort of frustration is often anger, which the two-year-old expresses as a temper tantrum. Frustration lurks in many corners of a toddler's life: imagine being big enough to want to run free but lacking the judgment to be allowed to. Discipline functions as those external boundaries; thoughtful discipline steps in when the toddler is fast approaching those boundaries and offers an alternative, a new activity, or a change of scenery.

Trying to divert your toddler before the temper tantrum is firmly entrenched should not be confused with denying that the child has negative feelings. Acknowledging the feelings and encouraging the child to voice them—without biting, punching, or other aggressive behavior—helps the child learn the difference between feelings and actions: feelings are always acceptable; aggressive actions are not. Developing self-control means that you don't have to act on your feelings, no matter how strong they are. As the child grows older, control of verbal aggression becomes the new target, but the foundations of self-control built in toddlerhood make that task easier.

One pitfall that some parents fall into is that they cannot bear to see their child unhappy, even for a few moments, and so they spend a lot of energy trying to keep him happy or at least looking as if he were having a good time. It is uncomfortable to see your child outright miserable, of course, but overanxious parents may prevent their child from experiencing even the small unhappinesses of life by giving in or "bribing" the child. It is important to remember that it is the minor discomforts and disappointments that help us build up a tolerance for the normal pains of life; to insulate children from all pain is to deprive them of the easiest way to learn to cope.

The negative side of overprotectiveness is that it may be used to satisfy the parent's inappropriate emotional needs by keeping the child overly dependent. One way to determine if you are being unsuitably protective or are properly cautious is to look at the situation and ask yourself what behavior on your part will encourage your child's independence and maturation, within the bounds of safety and sensibility. If, for instance, you are debating whether your two-year-old should be able to run ahead of you on a walk down a street where a strange dog is lurking unleashed, safety would dictate that you keep a firm hand on your little one; but if it is a question of allowing him to climb up a small ladder and slide down a sliding board alone, it may be creating unnecessary fear and dependence to insist on carrying him up and sliding down together. In the first case, a strange dog is a real threat (to adults as well as to inquisitive toddlers), but while it is possible that the child may fall in the playground, to go beyond the logical precautions (equipment of appropriate size to the child's size and ability and in good condition, no hazards in the immediate area) may be stultifying to the development of the child's self- control. Overcoming the natural apprehension of trying a new activity helps activate the child's sense of power over his environment and increases his self-confidence.

Part of self-confidence is being aware of your feelings about a situation and using this self-knowledge to your advantage. This has become all the more evident in recent years as information about child molestation has become more widespread and parental awareness has increased. What researchers have found is that the traditional teachings about not accepting candy from strangers has been useless in helping the majority of young victims; often, they say, the perpetrator is someone the child knows. Since most victims have been taught to fear strangers but not to be aware of and voice their discomfort when they are molested by family members or familiar people, the incidence of these crimes has been greatly under-reported, the result being youngsters growing up with the feeling that they were not protected against the very person they were taught to trust. The self-confident child who is sure of his parents' love and trust will not be afraid of telling; politeness will take a backseat to self-preservation when the child seems threatened and he will "yell and tell." He will be true to himself, and this self-trust will extend to trustworthiness and, for those whom he deems trustworthy, trustful feelings.

Discipline, guidance, boundary-setting, all require listening: (really listening, not just pretending) to your child, to your partner, and, perhaps most important, to yourself. Your own sense of self-control is a model for your child. If your behavior is fairly consistent, if you take the initiative in a situation rather than wait for something to respond to, and if you demonstrate confidence in your actions, your child has an excellent role model. If you have had problems with self-control and confidence since your own childhood, the miracle of parenting is that you can use this time of teaching and leading your child to give yourself a refresher course in self-discipline, this time as both teacher and student. Listening to your own inner feelings will give you the answers you need.

Couples also need to listen to each other's inner feelings with caring and respect. You won't always be able to present a united front to your children, or want to. Sometimes, in fact, the best thing you can teach your child is that a loving couple can disagree. You are both individuals, needing each other's support in parenting rather than mindless, automatic agreement. As long as the basic philosophy is the same, minor differences in style can work themselves out.

Discipline is a joint effort between both parents and the child, making communication essential. Developing a mutual style of discipline should start even before parenthood, when the goals for family life are first being formulated; the philosophy will continue to grow and evolve as the individuals and the family pass through the stages to maturity.

May our child grow with faith in us
As we have grown with faith in You.
Please grant us patience for ourselves,
For each other, for our child.
And let us learn Your lesson clear:
To listen with an open heart.

Growing

Three years is a delightful age: after a year of living with a toddler whose vocabulary seems to be ninety percent "No!", suddenly you are blessed with a young person who is much more a child than a baby. He speaks in complete sentences most of the time, and his eating and sleeping habits more closely approximate those of the rest of the family. He looks more an adult as his body proportions change from the relatively large head and chest of infancy to the more elongated arms and legs of childhood. His coordination has developed to the point where he can ride a tricycle, feed himself neatly, and dress and undress, except for buttoning and tying shoelaces.

The three-year-old's parents have grown, too; they are now more relaxed and confident of their abilities. Having gone through the period of adjustment to family life, their spiritual bonds are more intense. Parents and child are used to each other, a familiarity that breeds not contempt but consideration and regard.

The years from three to five are often referred to as the preschool years; in fact, most children attend some sort of organized program during this time, be it a formal preschool class, an informal playgroup, or day care. As more mothers join the work force, the demand for these services rises, and often insufficient consideration is given to what type of care is best for each child.

In order to cope well with a preschool environment, the child has to have matured to the point where he can tolerate the necessary amount of separation from the parents; preschool classes generally have one adult to each eight or ten children, which limits the amount of time that the child can realistically expect to spend in a one-to-one encounter with the teacher, so the child must be secure enough to postpone some needs.

Day-care centers, preschools, church-sponsored daycare groups, and nurseries may vary widely in the type of actual teaching they offer, but all group care situations require that the child adapt to sharing and taking turns with playmates. Some children readily share and enjoy cooperative play, while others need to control their belongings (and possibly other children's too), since they feel how little control they have over their lives.

Children, lacking mature judgment, need to be protected from accidents that frequently occur when large groups have little supervision; this requires that they obey the teachers and follow directions. This is difficult for many children whose curiosity may be squelched by an adult who misinterprets it as mischievousness.

The most important factor in choosing a preschool is the philosophy of the institution and how close it is to the parents' feelings about child-rearing. It is a good idea to visit the school you are considering for your child and observe the children. Are they spontaneous and smiling? Do they appear satisfied with themselves? Or do they seem to have lost what makes each one of them unique? Have you checked the staff's qualifications and credentials? Children are born individually (even multiple births are individuals), not in litters, and they need to be in the company of adults who see what is special about each one and who nurture that God-given singularity. They need to have real work, not just time-consuming but unstimulating coloring books and television. They need to exercise their large muscles, their small muscles, their brains, and their interaction skills.

The best alternative for a less mature child whose parents are both working full-time may be a caretaker combined with a playgroup, to provide the right mixture of individual attention and group activity. An informal playgroup, usually consisting of four to six parents and children, is an alternative to full-time day care, which can also be used by parents who don't work outside the home. These groups generally work as cooperative projects, with two parents taking the role of teacher each time the group meets. A group that meets three times a week, perhaps for two hours each time, gives each parent four free hours a week without having to pay for a babysitter. Some groups take additional children into the group and allow their parents to contribute money for equipment supplies, snacks, and trips in lieu of the expected contribution of time.

Of course, the ultimate decision must be based on what is available that meets the family's needs, but for most parents there will be some level of choice. Under the pressure of needing to make some reliable arrangements for their child's care during their working hours, some parents may contract with the school that promises to be a complete substitute for the family, teaching not only preparation for reading skills and creative arts, but moral training too. While school may provide a good supplement to what the child learns at home, it can never be a substitute for the parents passing on their family philosophy.

Morals are taught by example, by the family, within the family. The virtues of patience and tolerance for others are taught by the parents who are kind to all people, while fear and prejudice are passed on by those who are narrow-minded and dogmatic. Parents' respect for themselves, each other, their child, and others reflects in their child's self-respect and consideration for others; and so it is with their disrespect.

The resurgence of interest in manners, marked by the renewed popularity of books on etiquette, has paralleled the reawakening of spiritual interests over the past decade. Perhaps this is because manners are really morality in action, a way to show what you truly believe in. Teaching children manners is a simple matter of having good manners yourself, not the pinky-in-the-air tea-drinking sort of manners but the kind that would never knowingly hurt anyone's feelings. Being sensitive to the type of situation that requires manners your young child may never have encountered before and providing the information needed to navigate, help him feel comfortable around all people.

For instance, most preschoolers who have been raised around able-bodied people are at a loss when they meet someone with physical limitations or someone whose appearance is markedly different from that of the family's usual companions. If they have not been taught that different is bad, they may just ask why that person is carrying a cane or sitting in a wheelchair. If they feel fear when they meet someone they perceive as radically dissimilar, either because they have sensed fear in their parents or because they have been threatened with physical harm, they may run away or make rude remarks.

One way to prepare your child for the eventuality of their meeting someone they may see as scary is to talk with him about the natural variety of human beings and how even though they may look or sound different, they are spiritual beings, God's children, just as we are, and we must respect His love for them by recognizing their humanity and treating them accordingly. Children need to understand that physical disabilities are not punishments for bad thoughts but are either the results of accidents or may have occurred before the person was even born. The curious child who wants to know why God allowed this to happen may simply be told that the person's soul is whole and that is what is important to God.

Adults often tell what they term "white lies" in social situations rather than hurt someone's feelings by telling the truth (white lies often have to do with situations that the person being lied to can't change—an unattractive nose or too uneven haircut, perhaps). Eventually all children pick up the social conventions, saying polite thank yous for gifts they really don't like and saying they have other plans when asked to go someplace they'd rather not, but in the preschool years, trying to teach the difference between "good" lies and "bad" lies doesn't work. Firstly, children in that stage don't have a clear understanding of the difference between reality and imagination. Secondly, they can't distinguish between good lies and bad ones. Finally, they become very confused if they are told always to tell the truth to their parents and are then asked by their parents to lie to someone else.

The best solution is, again, be a good role model for your child and tell the truth. Remember that three, four, and five year olds are literal-minded and will take what you say as the truth, no matter how outlandish, so don't tease them with tales of bogeymen coming to steal them away if they're bad. Also, don't count on them to cover for you by answering the phone and saying you're in the shower when you're not: you'll only be teaching your child to lie to you.

A child's conception of reality differs so much from that of an adult that what is decidedly abnormal for adults is perfectly acceptable for children: adults who talk to creatures who aren't there are usually diagnosed as having a mental illness, schizophrenia, while preschoolers who do the same are allowed to have imaginary friends. While the presence of imaginary friends may be a bit disconcerting to parents, especially when they are asked to set an extra place at the table or not to sit in a certain chair because their invisible (to adults) friend is occupying it, it is most emphatically not a symptom of present or future mental illness. It may, in fact, mean that the child has a vivid imagination and a creative mind, or it may just be that he has no real playmates and is lonely. In that case, going to a playgroup or nursery school may end the imaginary friendship, or the invisible pal may go along to help the child get over the strangeness of being in preschool and disappear when the child is comfortable with the new experience.

Real friends, on the other hand, present completely different problems. Because children mature at different rates, two playmates may be the same chronological age but have widely divergent social skills. Sometimes the slower one learns by imitating the quicker one, but just as often the reverse happens and your child returns from playgroup or a neighbor's yard with a whole new set of fears, mannerisms, or "dirty" or "curse" words.

The best way to discourage the use of bad language is to state calmly that those words are not part of your family's vocabulary and that you don't expect to hear them repeated. Those words are interesting only when they provoke a response, so it's best to ignore them rather than scold or, even worse, laugh or otherwise encourage repetition. The same is true for mannerisms, that is, the silly faces that children imitate (and think are hilarious).

Fears are another matter. They are quite common among preschoolers and come in many different forms. Some are caused by a frightening experience—for instance, a very large dog barking menacingly at the child. Other fears seem to be an expression of the general anxiety present in the child's life: they are more a peg to hang everyday stress on. These may change frequently and eventually disappear as the child grows older.

Where the child has developed a specific fear—say of clowns (anything that distorts human features, such as masks, makeup, or deformities, is often frightening to this age group)—the best approach may be to try to avoid the feared object until the child is older and more sophisticated. Later on, the source of fear can be approached gently with a lot of parental support, perhaps by reading a story about the feared object or looking at pictures together. Only after the child has become desensitized to the dreaded thing should it be approached closely. Trying to force the child to confront the fear while it is still very powerful will not cure it: more likely the fear will intensify.

The opposite of fear is trust: for the child this means trusting his parents and, through them, trusting God. The basic security that the infant learns to count on grows into the preschooler's confidence in his parents to protect him from outside threats and from his impulses. In turn, this trust in his parents will form the foundation for his eventual understanding of his spiritual self and his relationship to his Creator.

The child's trust is still fragile at this stage of life; although he seems to crave independence at times, parents need to remember that self-reliance and self-sufficiency can develop only where the child is secure in the knowledge that he is not being pushed and can retreat to a more dependent stance when the need arises.

It is equally true that trying to keep the growing child dependent long past the time he needs a tight rein may create and sustain additional fears, without the child having the freedom in which to face those fears and overcome them.

How will we know
When to hold our child close,
When to open our arms,
When to let him go free?
As the birds nudge their young
From their place in the nest
In their heavenly time
By our faith we will see.

SCHOOLING

By the time your child is six years old or so, he will be spending a good part of each weekday in school. For some children, school will be a place of learning, mastering skills, and developing an appreciation for nature and the arts; for others, school will be a source of lifelong unpleasant memories. Parents can make schooling an enjoyable and valuable experience for their child by choosing a school carefully and actively participating in their child's education.

The type of school—public, private, or parochial—should be decided on as early as possible, even before the child is born, since the most sought-after schools often have waiting lists, or requirements such as belonging to the sponsoring church or organization for a specific number of years before an application is taken. Family philosophy should be the primary consideration in choice of school system, although the final choice of school will be determined by geographical and economic considerations.

Different school systems have different goals: the only way to find out what the school's educational objectives are is to ask the director or principal, keeping in mind that an objective is not a promise or guarantee. Another point to remember is that school is not the only place of learning and that the home continues to be the strongest influence for many more years. If, for instance, religious training is very important to the family and the parents feel that they can give their child adequate spiritual education at home and in their own church, a nondenominational school that provides a well-rounded secular education with the emphasis on the basic skills of reading and mathematics may be the preferred choice.

No matter what the stated objectives or curriculum of a school, the individual teacher will have the greatest influence on the child. Since most school systems have some sort of tenure arrangement whereby anyone teaching the required number of years is guaranteed to be kept on, whether or not the students are learning, parents should meet with whoever will be teaching their child's class. This holds true for private and public schools; most schools will try to accommodate parents who are dissatisfied with their child's teacher by arranging a conference, or, if unavoidable, a transfer to another class. Teachers are human, after all, and may have preferences they are not aware are expressing themselves in how they interact with your child.

Although there have always been parents who have preferred to teach their children themselves, it is only relatively recentlythat there has been a home schooling movement. More and more parents are rejecting formal schooling, preferring to set their own priorities for their child's education and training. While home schooling does give parents closer control over what their child is taught, it is difficult for parents who lack the necessary preparation and/or time.

Regardless of which system is chosen, parents still retain the responsibility for seeing that their child is learning. They need to help their child develop the habits that encourage learning, and regular attendance is the first of these.

Starting school, especially if the child has had no preschool or playgroup experience, can be frightening to the young child. Playing school at home is a good way to prepare your child for some of the new experiences he will encounter, like having to follow rules and procedures. Many kindergartens have a "get-acquainted" day before the actual opening of school to familiarize the new students with the school building and personnel. Knowing where he will sit, which hook to hang his sweater on, and where the bathroom is adds much to the child's feelings of belonging.

Some children develop a real fear of going to school because of older children's scary stories or because they have misinterpreted something that happened to them at school. A child with school phobia may complain of pains in the morning that disappear as soon as the school bus has left or may cry to be allowed to stay at home. Most experts feel that the cause is anxiety over being separated from the mother, and they agree that the worst way to deal with the problem is to give in to the child's demands. Some experts suggest that many mothers of school-phobic children actually encourage their demands out of their own insecurity. Whatever the cause, missing school is ultimately detrimental to the child's socialization with his classmates as well as a hindrance to learning, so if the problem persists, it should be discussed with the teacher.

By the time your child goes off to school he should have a place to organize his homework and school papers. This doesn't have to be a formal desk: sturdy cartons can be transformed into bookcases and file boxes. He also needs a quiet place to read and do written work. Again, there's no need to redecorate; merely let your child know that his schoolwork is important and that it deserves the proper attention. Work habits are learned best by imitation, so setting a good example by clearing away your work when you are finished is the most eloquent lesson you can give.

Another important lesson that is best learned at home is how to schedule your time. Having a fairly consistent set of routines for mealtimes, bedtime, homework, recreation, and chores makes it easier to organize the household, with plenty of time left over for spontaneous family fun. Having a special time (or times) for family prayer or devotions every day communicates to your child that God is in your family's life every day, not just on Sundays.

Giving your child regular chores—real work, not make-work—is another part of learning. Whether you choose to link chores with spending money or with teaching the laws of free-market economics or prefer to instill a sense of pleasure at being helpful to others, is a family decision. Regardless, the child needs to understand the basics of a job well done. (Including cleaning up after the job is done!)

The connection should be made right from the beginning between the child's actions and the consequences. For example, the child may be expected to help keep the house neat but standards to be decided upon by the family and communicated. This doesn't mean the child can't scatter toys around during imaginative play or spend a morning finger-painting on the kitchen table. It merely means that he is expected to return to its former state the area of the home he has used for his pleasure so that other family members may use it. Taking personal responsibility for small duties now helps prepare the child to assume larger tasks later. It cannot be overemphasized that teaching this sort of responsibility can be accomplished only if the parents act as role models.

It is tempting to do things yourself rather than watch your child struggle and not produce as good a result as you could yourself. But to take over for him is to cheat him of the opportunity for successful completion of the job. Here is where parents need a lot of patience!

Homework can be either an important supplement to your child's school day or just another task to be completed as quickly as possible: The difference is how you feel about it. Where the family emphasis is on schooling as a credential for a future job and the important achievements are measured in diplomas and degrees, the temptation is great to assist the child so that homework and papers are perfect, and the report card reflects all A's. But where learning is revered for what it is—power, enlightenment, and glory—the joy of self-discovery is what parents want their child to gain from school.

While homework should be the child's job alone (if the child doesn't understand the homework, the parent's helping may mask the child's need to have the material expanded on in the classroom), there are many parent-child activities that enhance learning. Playing games together and having the child keep score is a good way to strengthen math skills; word games help with spelling (keep a dictionary handy to resolve disputes) and reading. Shopping is a chore when done alone but a shared learning experience when the list is made by the child and, as multiplication and division are introduced, he helps determine the best prices. Very young children can get into the habit of sending letters to faraway relatives: the child draws pictures and dictates the letter at first and graduates to writing the letter and addressing the envelope as he grows. What starts as a game easily becomes a habit as the pleasure of correspondence is learned. And, unless the recipient prefers it, texting or email is just not the same.

It's important for parents to maintain their early involvement in their child's school. Becoming part of the local parent or parent and teacher association and attending school programs alerts the family to curriculum changes, new programs, and special activities. Volunteering to be a class parent or helping with school projects gives you an open opportunity to communicate your expectations for your child to teachers and administrators. An added bonus is that young children are usually proud to see their parents helping around their school: working with the school helps it work for your child.

One of the major issues in education that seem to swing from one extreme to the other with great frequency is that of grades and report cards. Some years the norm is the old-fashioned letter grades; other times it is pass or fail. Whichever it is, report cards often cause conflict among parent, child, and school because of misunderstandings about what they are supposed to be reports on.

Standardized test scores are similar to report cards in that they, too, cause confusion and disturbance, as they are abstract measures of a real person, your child. You should ask your child's teacher what the grades and scores are used for. If they are given only because state law requires them, but the school does not put much stock in their value as evaluators or predictors of your child's chances for success in adulthood, they should be of little concern.

However, if standardized tests are used to determine the child's placement in a slower or faster class and you know that the score does not accurately reflect your child's abilities, then you should go to the school administrator and request a reevaluation.

A good school administrator knows that the parents' perception of their child often has more validity than a computer-scored pencil-and-paper test. A good teacher knows how to use that parent-child bond to create the most conducive atmosphere for effective learning.

Please bless those who teach our child
As they reflect the light of knowledge;
May their minds be ever open
To the beauty of Your world.
Let them see the child before them
Glorifying Your creation
And with caring hearts and hands
Guide him toward Your sacred goal.

Adapting

It has often been said that the only constant thing in life is change. It follows, then, that the ability to adapt—to be able to adjust to new situations as they arise—is a valuable tool for life. It's a quality that comes naturally to some children but is a hard-learned lesson for others.

Most children's first major experience with change occurs when they are presented with a new baby brother or sister. Suddenly, their mother and father are less available and visitors who once sought them out first now come to see the new baby. It's a perfect setup for the development of rivalry and jealousy, but also for the encouragement of tolerance and cooperation.

There is never a convenient time to have a baby. With natural child spacing, babies do tend to come about two or three years apart, but that is just an average, not a guarantee. One couple, practitioners of natural family planning but with a dozen children spaced no more than a year apart, just tells those rude enough to ask, "God sends them; we take them." They maintain that the closeness in age doesn't cause jealousy until the newest baby gets big enough to get into the older children's treasures, and that even with the need to get in line to shower in the morning, the older children would rather have a new brother or sister for Christmas than anything else. They have learned to value people over things, and that is an important lesson indeed.

Getting siblings to cooperate instead of fight is every parent's dream. Some go overboard, attempting always to be fair, forgetting that life isn't fair. In their insistence that all their children be treated equally and at all times receive the same portion, they inadvertently downplay the individual nature of each one. Other parents give in to the urge to compare one child to another, driving a wedge between the two that lasts a lifetime.

It's important to treat the impending arrival of a new sibling as a natural, desirable occurrence. Some parents make the mistake of asking the first child if he would like a new brother or sister, despite the fact that the pregnancy has already occurred and, like it or not, there will soon be a baby in the house. A better approach is to tell the child as soon as the pregnancy is well under way and include him in the preparations.

One of the most traumatic features of having a new sibling is the separation from the mother when she goes to the hospital to give birth. Many families choose home birth or a birth center or hospital that allows the child to be present at the birth and/or visit the mother and newborn immediately after. Where this is impossible, preparing the child well in advance for the mother's possibly sudden departure is important. If a familiar person can stay with the child throughout his mother's hospitalization, the additional pressure of having to adapt to a new caretaker is minimized.

Another source of disturbance is that the older child may now be expected to share not only his parents but his room. While it may be essential due to space considerations, the problem of how to divide the space should be determined by family consensus. Sharing a room can, by necessity, enhance cooperation, but only if the child whose room it originally was does not feel displaced. Some space, no matter how small, should be designated private for each child. Knowing that there is a secret place that no one will go into without permission makes living in a growing family easier.

Having a pet can be a safety valve for the older child's inevitable moments of jealousy, especially if it is a breed that is tolerant of children's cuddling. Unlike the traditional baby doll given to the new big brother or sister, an animal needs and responds to the child's care. It's best to adopt the pet before the new baby is born, so that the relationship between animal and child has had time to solidify and so the care routines are set. A veterinarian or qualified breeder is a good source of information on what kind of pet is best suited to the child's age group and natural style.

As children mature, their individual ways of being will determine how close or far apart they want to be. While it is impossible for parents to make siblings want to play together, it is remarkably easy to set one against the other. The most divisive tactic is to take one child's side against the other, yet parents often do this without thinking, out of their protective feelings toward the younger child. This upsets the balance of power between the siblings considerably: the favored child, able to lean on the parent's support, fails to develop a workable defensive posture, while the older child ends up angry at both the younger sibling and the parent. Because anger at his parent is unthinkable—"if mother and father know I'm angry at them, won't that make them angry at me?" he reasons—the child feels guilty. The guilt feeds the anger and the anger feeds the guilt in a vicious cycle until frustration builds to an intolerable level.

While parents shouldn't take sides in sibling squabbles, neither can they allow the stronger one to get his way constantly. Sometimes the only solution is a negotiated truce with an enforced period of separation. The primary point is to allow siblings to work out their relationship without too much interference but with a lot of support and guidance. Here, too, parental example speaks louder than sermons: if you and your spouse bicker over petty issues, don't expect your children to learn the gentle art of peacemaking.

Parent-child conflicts are generally more serious than sibling skirmishes. Children, even with age gaps of several years, are on the same level: they are all dependent on their parents for survival. When the dispute is between parent and child, there is a built-in lopsidedness to the balance of power.

It's important to get to the root of parent-child conflict. Sometimes it is just an honest difference of opinion on a specific issue, but constant arguing is often an expression of another emotion or of a long-standing situation that has not been openly acknowledged.

Even very young children are aware when all is not well with their parents. Whether the problems are financial, like sudden unemployment or bankruptcy, or have to do with the parents' marriage, the change in tension level in the household is readily reacted to by the children. Even with severe, life-threatening illness, it is better to tell than to try to hide the cause of concern.

Some parents are shocked to discover the intensity of their child's emotions, especially when a friend or family member is very ill or dies. The child may appear distressed for a few moments and then go back to playing. This can be upsetting for the mourning adult, who may believe this behavior indicates disrespect on the part of the child. But this is the way that children deal with tragedy, by absorbing it bit by bit, as their emotional tolerance allows. The child who is unable to take the mourning in slow stages becomes overwhelmed, much like an adult does, and can become seriously depressed.

In the case of marital discord, the threat of divorce or desertion can be as distressing to the child as death. Here the guilt comes from the child wishing for the parents to stay together and, at the same time, wanting them to stop fighting, which may happen only if they separate. The child is further hurt by any demands that he side with one parent against the other.

Death or divorce is upsetting to the child on a spiritual level too. If he has been taught to place his faith in God and then perceives that God is not answering his prayers, he may experience a crisis of faith, much like an adult might in the same situation. In such instances it may be helpful for the child as well as the parents to talk to a minister or pastoral counselor who is trained to deal with emotional distress within the framework of the family's beliefs and values.

Whether change is essentially positive, as in the case of a new sibling, or negative—illness, death, or divorce, it brings with it, for adult and child alike, a confrontation of feelings and, often, the reassessment of cherished values. Refusing to adapt or adapting in unproductive ways leads only to despair; confronting the pain of change with the determination to master it presents the opportunity for the renewal of faith on a deeper, more passionate level.

Teach us, O Lord, to bend to Your will
As the grasses bow before the wind:
With roots held close within the earth
Though tempest whip the tendrils fine.
Let prayer and consolation heal
The petty hurts our lives sustain:
Our faith, though challenged by our fears
Grows steadfast in our hearts and minds.

Maturing

Many decades ago, when it was assumed that the children would follow the parents into the family business, working and learning the job was an important part of childhood. Whether they were farmers or merchants, craftsmen or laborers, one of the obligations of parents was to ensure that their children would be able to survive as adults. Now, with the spectrum of vocational choice broadening to include jobs that the parents have never even heard of, the emphasis on parental teaching has turned to what is euphemistically termed "family life education." But just as the public schools have almost universally taken over the responsibility for vocational preparation, so have they made inroads into fulfilling their students' needs for information on sexuality and other topics that many believe are the domain of the family.

Surveys have shown that while many parents are opposed to sex education in the schools, neither do they feel competent to teach their children about this very important part of life. Yet sex education begins at birth: the baby begins to learn the differences between mother and father right away. Later on, the parents' attitudes toward the human body are transmitted to the baby as they bathe and care for him. The lessons at this stage are nonverbal and mainly consist of helping the child develop healthy attitudes and self-confidence.

The infant's feelings and attitudes are reflections of those of his parents. As with other matters, it is often the unspoken opinions of the parents that come across the loudest, so if these feelings include discomfort or disgust for the human body and its sexual functions, it's best to explore these attitudes before passing them on to your children.

Later, as the child begins to want bathroom privacy for himself, he is ready to respect others' privacy needs. At this point most children begin to develop their own theories about how babies are born: most of these hypotheses follow the digestion mode, with which the child is familiar. They surmise that the mother eats something—a seed, in many versions—and the baby grows in her stomach; when the time is right she defecates and out comes the baby. Some children share their thoughts with their parents, expecting agreement or denial, while others ask straight out where babies come from. Others still never really ask but hint around, perhaps already aware that this is a sensitive subject. Many parents feel that discussions of reproduction are best left until the teenage years, but it cannot be overstated that sexuality is something we are born with; the correct information and positive attitudes are needed from childhood on.

It's important to have an open relationship with your child, one where he feels comfortable talking about personal matters with you. This isn't something that happens automatically when the need arises but stems from the earliest parent-child discussions. When the subject under discussion is sexuality, the first step is for the parents to feel comfortable with their own maleness and femaleness.

It's a good idea to find a book or online source of information on where babies come from long before the need arises; unfortunately, many available children's works treat what should be a serious subject with inappropriate humor, so read the book before you pay for it. It's helpful also to review the basic biology: although you aren't about to give a complicated lecture on human reproduction, it's a great parental confidence-builder to know that you can handle any question that arises.

Most children start asking about babies when they are about three years old; this may occur around the time their own mother, a relative, or a family friend is pregnant. Since the only experience they have with changing figures is that eating a lot of food can cause someone to grow large around the middle, they may approach the subject warily, asking if the pregnant woman has been eating too much. Whether they are forthright or shy about asking, children need to be given the information they are asking for. It's not necessary to sit down with a complex explanation of the entire process the very first time the question arises, but merely to answer what is asked.

For instance, when the three-year-old asks, "Where do babies come from?" a perfectly simple answer is they grow in a special place inside their mother. If the child then concludes that this must be the stomach, he can be told that it is not in the stomach, which is where the food we eat goes, but in another, special place. For the time being, that is enough information.

It often takes many repetitions of the simplest fact until the child is ready to go on to the next logical question, how does the baby get out? In fact, it may be many months before that question arises. The simple answer is through a special passage that connects the special place where the baby grows to the outside. You can name the special places, but it is best to give the correct names instead of cute terms: the proper name for the place the baby grows is, of course, the uterus, and the passageway is the vagina. Using the correct terms from the beginning makes the whole education process more matter-of-fact.

By the time the child is four or five, he will know that the genitals are different for males and females and will begin to wonder what the father's part is in all this. If the genitals have been given their proper names, penis and vulva (which is the correct name for the part of the female genitals that is visible: the vagina is not visible), the child can refer to them with dignity, and the parent is less likely to feel embarrassed or childish.

If the child has not asked questions by the time he reaches six or seven, it's a good idea to ask him if he knows how babies are born and then correct any misconceptions. If he says he does not know, ask him if he wants to know and if he says yes, proceed with the story.

While it may be confusing, and a little scary, for a three-year-old to be told that God puts the baby in the mother's uterus, by six the child can be told about pregnancy and birth within the context of God's plan for us to "be fruitful and multiply." The simplest answer to questions about the father's role is that the tiniest bit of life in the father, called the sperm, joins the tiniest bit of life in the mother, the ovum. It's best to avoid using the terms seed and egg, since they are easily confused with seeds for the garden and the eggs that are served at breakfast.

From the meeting of these tiny bits of life, a new baby starts to grow in the mother's uterus. The child can be told that it is God's plan that to have a baby there must be life from a man and life from a woman so that the baby will have a mother and a father. If the child's mother is pregnant, it should be explained that it takes a long time for the baby to grow big enough to be born and that during that time her body is also preparing to feed the baby after the birth.

Many local museums have exhibits on human reproduction; some may be appropriate for young children, but it's best for the parents to check first. There may be models of the baby growing within the uterus that show that even before birth it is indeed a human being.

The child may wonder how it is possible for such a large baby to get out of the mother's body, especially after seeing pictures or models. Again, it is best to be honest and say that it may be uncomfortable for a little while but that the passageway stretches to let the baby pass through and then gets smaller again. The child whose mother expects to go to the hospital for her next birth should be told that the mother isn't sick or having an operation, but that she may want to have some help giving birth and the doctors and nurses know how to assist. If the child is to be present at the next birth, whether this is to take place at home, in a birth center, or in a hospital, he needs to be fully prepared. Classes and visits to the midwife or doctor are highly recommended.

Again, the attitudes about sexuality and family life that are transmitted nonverbally are more powerful than books or classes, especially for the very young child. Although the depth of explanation will change with the maturity of the child, if the family's basic attitude is one of respect and reverence for their own and one another's humanity, they need not worry that their child will not be able to handle the information.

Somewhere around nine or ten years of age, all girls need to be taught about menstruation; since boys generally mature a year or two later, explanations of male maturity and nocturnal emissions ("wet dreams") can wait until ten or eleven. Children mature into adolescents on differing timetables, but it's best for the child to be prepared, even if the information turns out to be given several years before it's needed.

As with pregnancy and birth, the attitudes about menstruation the mother has (which doubtless were influenced by her own mother's attitudes) will be passed on, along with the verbal explanations, to her daughter, so it's a good idea to reevaluate your feelings about this womanly function before your daughter needs to be told.

Some observant girls will notice that their mother buys certain products at the drugstore at certain times of the month; some will be curious enough to ask what such things are for. Others may not ask questions until a friend begins to menstruate. But whether the questions come first or not, when the time comes to explain menstruation, the best approach is to present it as a natural part of life, not a curse (if this is the name her friends use for their menstrual periods) but a blessing, for it means her body is healthy and functioning normally.

Menstruation should be explained as part of the total reproductive process, part of God's plan to keep the earth populated. At the simplest level, it can be described as the monthly renewal of the lining of the uterus. It starts long before a girl is ready to become a mother so that her body will be accustomed to producing just the right amount of soft lining for a baby to grow in. Many girls will menstruate irregularly at first, perhaps several months elapsing between menstrual periods. This should be explained as her body going through a learning process.

Boys, too, at around the time they are told about their own sexuality, should be taught about how a girl matures. Girls should likewise have a general understanding of male sexuality.

Since the task of telling a son about his reproductive future generally falls to the father, he should first examine his own attitudes, perhaps reminiscing about what his own father told him. If he learned about sex from the boys in his neighborhood, perhaps he might think about what misinformation he might have received, how it affected his life, and how he would have liked to have been treated at that sensitive time. Male attitudes are transmitted nonverbally, just as female ones are: Be careful that what you say is what you mean. Double messages—the kind where the underlying attitude is at odds with what is being said—are confusing to everyone, but especially to children who lack the sophistication to sort out the conflicting bits.

Nocturnal emission can be explained as the body's natural response to the beginning of sperm production. Semen is ejaculated during sleep, or the boy may be awakened by the sensations. Either way, it is an indication that he is growing up normally, and that although he is not yet ready socially, emotionally, and spiritually to be a father, he is ready physically.

At the same time preadolescents are preparing for their entrance into adolescence, they may be experiencing insecurity about this inevitable step. For some, the body changes are frightening; for others, the responsibilities of growing up are overwhelming and the desire to stay a child is strong. This is the time for parents to encourage the child's self-regard. Where there is a choice between treating the preadolescent as a child or a young adult, it's best to err on the side of young adulthood, emphasizing that with the added responsibility of growing up there is also added reward and authority.

For parents, too, there are additional responsibilities as their children approach adolescence, but for the family where mutual respect and cooperation are cherished values, there is also joy and satisfaction.

Lend us Your wisdom, Lord,
In those moments when we feel
Inadequate to the task
Of raising our children;
And remind us that perfection
Need not be demanded
Of our children when You
Do not ask it of us.

Coping

All lives have their ups and downs: there are moments, like the birth of a baby, that are golden; there are the blessedly ordinary days when the good moments outnumber the bad; there are the sad days when life seems dreary; and there are days where we are overwhelmed by grief, anger, and disappointment.

Even infants have their ups and downs. The mild frustration of wanting to be fed yet having to wait for mother to unbutton or to prepare a bottle is their first lesson in coping.

Dismal days are often due to a loss or change. It may be loss of a cherished belonging or, more tragic, loss of a loved one; it may be loss of a friendship through misunderstanding or one family moving away; it may be the loss of status that comes with loss of employment or not being chosen for a desired job; or it may be the kind of loss of self-image that often accompanies disease or disability. Whatever the reason, the feelings and expression of grief are normal. Coping, however, is not measured in terms of normality. It is either effective or ineffective and is usually a reflection of our parents' style.

Children grieve, too, though this is not always obvious to adults. The reasons for their heartaches may seem silly or frivolous to their parents, and the tears are often brushed off with the admonition that big boys (or girls) don't cry. But small sorrows, it seems, are what teach us to deal with the certainty that we will have larger sorrows as we age. Forgetting how to cry makes it much more difficult to express grief and so prolongs the pain.

Whatever the reason for the reaction to grief, people respond in pretty much the same ways. In the most tragic circumstance, that of the sudden, unexpected death of a child, the first response is numbness, a sort of temporary anesthesia that allows the truth to sink in very slowly. Medical professionals who are uncomfortable with the emotions expressed at the time of loss often offer tranquilizers to help the grieving person over the worst hours. But God has mercifully provided the human being with a natural sedative, the numbness of denial, to dull the immediate pain.

The denial gradually passes and is replaced by feelings of anger and hostility, often directed at God for allowing the unthinkable to happen. The anger is blended with guilt and feelings of self-recrimination. The mourner may beseech God, begging Him to allow the deceased to return in exchange for his own life. If these feelings are verbalized, they can be resolved and the grief process can continue; if they are turned inward, they form the basis for emotional depression. The depressed person tends to isolate himself from others, turning away from all possible sources of comfort, and the anger-guilt-depression cycle becomes a permanent part of life.

The person who was not allowed to grieve over losses in childhood often relives the feelings of those earlier incidents while experiencing the new woe. If the rage and guilt remain unresolved, they may even lead to illness: the list of maladies that physicians believe are influenced by feelings is long. Other people just seem to be able to deny the effects of the loss. They put up a happy front and may fool even their closest friends and family into believing they have recovered from their loss, but the pain is there just below the surface of conscious thought.

If the grief is allowed expression, eventually it decreases to a tolerable level. In the case of the loss of a child, the process may take several years until the stage of acceptance is reached. Acceptance does not mean denying that the child ever existed or that the loss ever occurred, but that the parent has been able to accept that the unthinkable actually did happen and that life will go on.

The way of patience is difficult: to let go of the illusion that we control life and death and to fully appreciate that "this, too, will pass," takes much soul-searching. But dealing with mourning leads one to the realization that although we do not control our time on earth, we can do much to determine how we will feel about it and how we will choose to react to pain and sorrow.

We may even find a new depth of spirituality as a result of grieving openly.

It is important for the family who has experienced the death of one of its members to have some time to mourn together and some time to grieve alone, especially when some of the survivors are very young. Children often misinterpret their parents' efforts to cope with loss. In the parents' endeavor to spare their children pain, they may exclude them from the funeral or memorial service, reinforcing their sense of isolation. In addition, young children often have fantasies about death that include the return of the loved one as a sort of ghost that will haunt them. Children may even feel responsible for the death, especially if they had some negative thoughts about the deceased just prior to the death.

Bringing children to a cemetery has become increasingly acceptable as it becomes evident that they are helped in their grieving by the opportunity to view the finality of death. Of course, the child should be prepared for what will happen; it should also be explained that the other mourners may be very tearful and may not feel like playing with him.

Death can be explained in the context of life, that it is the end of earthly existence. It is fine to share your view of the afterlife with your child, but death should never be compared with temporary states, such as sleep. Grieving children may normally have some sleep disturbance; to add the fear of dying while asleep to the child's already overloaded mind will only increase insomnia.

With older children and adolescents, the subject of death may arise in a totally different context, that of suicide. At the time of the first edition of this book, suicide was the third leading cause of death among adolescents after accidents and homicide (and many of those deaths listed as accidental were probably consciously or unconsciously suicide), so the chances of a neighbor or schoolmate taking his own life are considerable. Since that time, suicide has surpassed accidents, although there is probably some overlap in that it can be difficult to sort out cause from outcome. The media often feature stories about suicide, leading to widespread awareness among teenagers. Whether that is positive or negative is also difficult to assess, since while there is increased awareness of the threat of suicide, it has also become somewhat 'normalized.' This creates less of a barrier to the teen who is in despair and cannot see another way out.

Most adolescents who commit suicide have had a long history of problems, starting in childhood and intensifying with age, often unacknowledged. They often feel isolated from other people, even though they may have many friends and caring families. Above all, they are children without hope, without the ability to see that even with all of life's pains, there is still much that makes it worthwhile.

Suicide prevention begins at home, by encouraging children to talk about their emotions, both negative and positive. Any threat or talk of intent to harm oneself must be taken seriously; many communities have crisis intervention counseling hotlines that can provide emergency help.

The coping method that is taught by the parents is not always an effective one, however. Some of the ineffective coping methods passed down from parent to child are aggression, panic, denial, and depression.

Aggression as a response to loss (whether it is an actual or threatened loss of a person or thing of value) may be expressed as demanding or even abusive behavior, destruction or manipulation of people or things, or withdrawal, "the silent treatment." Most abusive adults were abused when they were children: if this was your experience, you must first believe that with God's help, the cycle can be broken. You can then admit to yourself that you need someone else to help you work it through and commit to changing what is not easy to change.

Overcoming aggression is largely a matter of becoming assertive: learning to express your feelings with words, clearly communicating how your child's behavior makes you feel rather than calling him names and judging him. For example, some parents feel compelled to tell their teenagers who like to sleep late on weekends that they will never amount to anything. Leave the judging to a higher court ("Judge not, lest ye be judged") and instead let them know your true feelings: "I get annoyed when you sleep late because the housework must get done on the weekend and we need you to share the chores."

Praising your child's positive behavior with warmth and sincerity is also part of teaching assertion. The feedback reinforces his understanding of how his actions affect others and, for better or worse, their responses to him.

Anxiety is a normal expression of fear. Mild anxiety keeps us alert while driving or using machinery. But when anxiety is exaggerated into panic, which happens when the reality of the fear is distorted, it tends to prevent the sufferer from making well-reasoned decisions. Often, the panic attacks are accompanied by physical symptoms that mimic severe conditions, causing further anxiety.

If your reaction to every fright, disappointment, or blunder is panic, the message you are giving your child is that the world is an overwhelming place. If your child believes that you, his parents, are incapable of triumph over adversity, how can he, so obviously smaller and less powerful, ever hope to learn how?

With denial, the danger is in the double message. The parent simultaneously transmits to the child the verbal communication that everything is all right and the non-verbal communication that the parent is troubled. It's a kind of lying to yourself and others without really being consciously aware of what you are doing. Most people react to someone else's denial with confusion, as if what they are hearing and what they are seeing cannot possibly go together. As with panic, the problem is that the true source of emotional discomfort has not been acknowledged. If denial is your habitual response to negative emotions, you may need someone who can help you confront the mixed messages you are sending.

Depression is a form of unexpressed anger at a loss or failure that has been turned inward. There is a sense of emptiness, hopelessness, and helplessness, and often a crisis of faith. Depressed parents often isolate themselves, physically and emotionally, from their children, perpetuating the family's sense of loss.

Some people seem able to pull out of depression by forcing themselves to get involved with activities; in effect, they learn to be happy. There is some biological evidence that physical exercise helps the brain release chemicals that combat depression, so that may be part of the recovery process.

There is also evidence that the tendency toward depression as a non-coping method may be inherited; many psychiatrists believe that some people have an imbalance in their brain chemistry, which predisposes them to periodic depressions that can be treated with medication. If all else has failed to lift a depression, the appropriate route may be medical.

Your successful coping with the vicissitudes of life is a demonstration of faith and skill for your children, no matter what their age. Sharing your self-confidence shows them that you will not crumble in the face of adversity but will admit to your distressful feelings and overcome them.

Coping is learned in stages: the infant learns to cope with the occasional absence of the mother; the child learns to cope with new experiences; preadolescents must cope with peer pressure and learn to seek solutions to problems; and by adolescence, when all the coping mechanisms that have been learned before are fully effective, he must face the identity crisis of young adulthood. Coping is taught by the parents' example and is nurtured by the parents' confidence in their child.

Most of all, your children need to know that you will always be there for them, not hovering over them, not smothering them, but there where they can find you when they need a reference point for their own lives. Trusting that they will be able to cope with whatever life brings and instilling in them the self- trust that is central to the development of coping ability is an ongoing task of inspiring parenthood.

Lord, let the numbness pass;
Let the anger be dissolved;
Take the feeling from my heart
That You have forsaken me.
Teach me that You never give
More burden than a soul can bear;
Let me know with certainty
That "this, too, shall pass" is truth.

Guiding

Adolescence is the time between childhood and adulthood. A relatively modern invention, it consists of the years of gradual transition to maturity. A century ago, when children were considered to be like adults, only smaller, there was no prolonged stage of preparation. As soon as you could support yourself you were considered an adult, with all the rights and responsibilities thereof. Now, with longer mandatory schooling and a more complex society, teenagers are expected to be subservient to the family, like children, while they are also expected to be adaptable and productive, like adults. No wonder so many parents consider their child's adolescence the most challenging season of parenthood!

The tasks of an adolescent are threefold. First, making the transition from being dependent on parents to being fully independent and self-reliant. Second, developing a self-concept—to know who you are and what you believe in—and, also an adequate level of self-esteem. Finally, attaining enough skill in relating to other people so that you will not be socially isolated.

Adolescents need help to meet these challenges successfully. They get the guidance and feedback they seek from many sources, including friends, teachers, religious leaders, the media, and their parents. Parents' opinions often seem to come last, especially in matters deemed to be of interest to teenagers only, but to thrive in this evolving stage, adolescents need to see their parents as authority figures. Authority is used in the sense of expertise and should not be confused with authoritarian, which implies a dictatorial approach.

Once again, in this stage of development as in the previous ones, parental example speaks louder than words. If their authority is based on rational judgments made by examining all available alternatives and choosing the best, they pass on to their adolescent respect for knowledge and clear thinking. On the other hand, if the parents tend to go along with what others have chosen for them, they will be unable to encourage any initiative their teenager exhibits.

The drive toward self-sufficiency is enhanced at school by gradually turning over to the young adolescent many of the responsibilities that were shared in childhood. By high school, completing homework assignments is the student's job alone: the parents' place is to be a sounding board for the new ideas their child is learning, not to keep track of project schedules. The responsibility for getting up early enough to have breakfast and get to school on time is the child's. (Children who like being woken up by a parent instead of an alarm clock are at a distinct disadvantage unless they intend to live at home the rest of their lives.)

Adolescents need to have achieved a reasonable level of self-reliance before they can be allowed adult privileges, especially those, like taking driving lessons, that require mature judgment. One way to assess adolescent judgment is to discuss items about teenage behavior that appear in the media, asking your child how he would have acted (similarly or differently) and why. A mature level of thought is marked by the ability to use reasoning to link an act and its possible consequences.

Another area in which teenagers may want to show their emerging maturity is vocational choice. Many adolescents hold after-school jobs that help them pay for college as well as get a taste of adult responsibility, but some use the job as an excuse to let studies go; the job becomes a means to getting money for immediate gratification of the desire for things rather than as a base for future accomplishment. Parents may find it difficult to distinguish their child's motivation, but a decline in school performance shortly after starting a job is a clue that this adolescent may not be ready to tackle any more work than that demanded by home and school.

Every adolescent goes through a process of growing self-awareness. Some call it the identity crisis; it is a time for reevaluating everything you believe in, including everything your parents taught you to believe in. Often this means that teenagers question the family's faith, not to destroy it but to demand of the parents that they help them understand the basis for their beliefs. In their active search for information they may express the desire to visit churches of faiths other than that of the family. Again, this is not a challenge but part of the spiritual search that all thinking human beings go through, so it is best to allow it to continue while holding fast to your own beliefs.

One of modern parents' great fears is that their child will not only reject the family's religion but will join another one, especially one deemed a cult. It's important for parents to understand that the adolescents who are attracted to the cults are generally more alienated than their peers; without strong parental involvement in their lives, teenagers often lack a sense of direction and latch on easily to the identity of the group they join. The child who feels free to question his parents and whose parents respond with interest, respect for their child's thoughts, and a nonjudgmental attitude is likely to have a high degree of self-confidence and self-worth. Being accepted by your own family makes the search for a family substitute unnecessary.

Another major parental concern is the widespread availability and use of alcohol and drugs. Some families do not drink at all, while for others, wine is part of ceremonial events only. For children growing up in these families, alcohol has no part or only a very small one in their image of adult life. But children who are raised in homes where binge drinking to the point of intoxication is the norm, whether it is a once-in-a-while occasion or an everyday event, are likely to see alcohol as an adult indulgence and end up imitating the behavior.

If ceremonial wine is part of the family's culture, there is no harm in allowing even a young child to have a sip at the proper time; the association between alcohol and family spiritual celebration is set in the child's mind and he accepts its infrequent, moderate use as normal. Overindulgence, at any age, is evidence of poor judgment.

Drugs, like alcohol, diminish judgment; further, they alter perception to such a great degree that though they may not be fatal themselves, they may lead to such poor decision-making that they endanger the life of the user. Chronic drug users, like chronic alcoholics, are often so unhappy with their lives that they use their drug (alcohol is a drug too) as a form of anesthesia. On a spiritual level, this is tragic, because it is a waste of the time we are allotted on earth, a misusing of our humanity.

Discovering that their child has fallen prey to drugs or alcohol is distressing for parents, who may suffer an enormous amount of guilt or may destroy their own relationship by blaming each other. If this is occurring in a family, they need to get help as soon as possible, even if their child is unwilling to cooperate. Many churches sponsor Alcoholics Anonymous groups, which accept those with drug problems, too, and many also have Al Anon meetings for the families to learn how to cope. Alcoholics Anonymous (in some communities there are chapters of Narcotics Anonymous, which operates in the same way) considers the problem holistically, knowing that successful treatment depends on healing the spirit as well as the body and mind.

Developing self-knowledge and developing relationships with others are interrelated tasks: one must have self-knowledge to give oneself fully in a relationship, and at the same time, a satisfying relationship lets us learn more about ourselves as we learn about the other person. Most teenagers start to socialize in groups long before they begin to pair off and date. The other group members provide feedback on how the adolescent rates in relation to his peers. This peer pressure can be negative if the peer group rewards antisocial behavior, or it can be positive, reinforcing the good qualities that the parents have modeled for their child.

At the point at which peer influence becomes as strong as family influence, some parents may feel that they are fighting an uphill battle. But this is a necessary step on the adolescent's way to adulthood; the best any parent can do is stay on the sidelines, cheer their teenager on, and be available when the need arises.

Sometimes the teenager's greatest need is for the firm, parental "No!" especially when friends are urging him to participate in an activity he has the insight to know he's not ready for but lacks the social confidence to back away from. Adolescents feel secure knowing their parents, while not wanting to overprotect them, are concerned enough about their welfare to use parental veto power when absolutely necessary.

Adolescence is the time when parents need to recognize the good things they did for their child, the loving care and concern, the leadership and support they provided, and the many hours of just being there for him. Although they can take neither credit nor blame for what their child will become, for that is between the child and his Creator, they can take pleasure and pride in knowing that they gave freely of themselves; that, after all, is what counts the most.

Help us, O Lord,
As we try to prepare
Our child for a world
We are never to see.
How can we guide him
Into the unknown?
With Your infinite vision
Lighting the way.

Emancipating

Eventually, the tasks of adolescence are mastered, and children move beyond the family, beyond the peer group, to take their rightful places in adult society. They are ready to commit to their work or calling and have developed their own value system, which allows them to form intimate, loving relationships. They are living away from their parents' home, perhaps at college or with a roommate or two, able to care for their personal needs, and able to begin to care for another's as well. When they return home to visit, it is as an equal; their peer group has enlarged to include all the adults they know.

Still, there are ambivalences. When your young adult's grandfather was his age, he was working and probably supporting a young family; there was no prolongation of dependency as is necessary when education extends many years past the eighteenth birthday. This period, which may continue until age twenty-six or later if graduate or professional school dictates, creates conflict in the post-adolescent, who, at the same time, needs to be treated as an adult, but is still considered a student, an adolescent.

For parents, there are other conflicts. One major area is how much financial support they should give to their child for higher education. While seventy-five years ago the general expectation was that parents would support their offspring though high school graduation, fifty years ago college attendance began to be viewed as a right and necessity. Now, with even college graduate level jobs becoming scarcer and promotion rarer in some fields, the graduate or professional degree is becoming the standard. With government-backed loans becoming more difficult to qualify for and tuition costs rising faster than the cost of living, adult children are finding themselves in the unenviable position of having to turn to their families for financial assistance.

While many parents have the means and welcome the opportunity to help, it is all too easy to attach strings to the loan or gift that have little or nothing to do with academics. These strings may be openly discussed; for instance, giving tuition for a specific course of learning that will lead to self-sufficiency but not for random classes in a field that is difficult to earn a living from. In some cases, the strings may be attached to hidden, undisclosed goals. These may include the assumption that the child will care for his parents in their old age. Although unspoken agreements may be understood by both sides, it's still a good idea to get things written down to avoid future conflicts.

In some families, tuition payments are treated as sort of an allowance, contingent on "good behavior." This situation can lead to the parents feeling they have to monitor their child's every move as they did when he was much younger, especially in the area of sexual behavior.

The issue of whether or not to have sexual relations before marriage has never been so difficult. In past times, people married at a younger age, around the time their desire for, and ability to sustain, a marital relationship coincided. Fears of pregnancy and venereal disease kept sexual behavior at a minimum, and virginity was the expected state at marriage, at least for the woman. Abortion was considered a sin, with no exceptions and, even if available, was often performed by an unqualified individual: sterility or death were real possibilities.

The sexual revolution of the 1960s changed the rules somewhat, at least in the more liberal areas of the country. The easy availability of birth control devices (often given free at college health services) and the subsequent legalization of abortion took much of the fear of nonmarital sex away from young adults. What remained were the personal aspects: while casual sex might be pleasurable, even exciting, it was not part of a more profound, more spiritual bond.

With the restraints against premarital sex lifted completely by the early seventies, many college students faced peer pressure as well as their own desires; student dissent with the "establishment" and the ready availability of drugs on many campuses made it even more difficult for those with religious ethics that forbade indulgence.

The beginning of the eighties seemed to bring a new concern to this age group, that of how they were going to earn enough money to ensure that they would lead the same good life they saw their parents lead. At the same time, promiscuous sex seemed to be headed for cultural annihilation. Some feel that the two were related, that students discovered that a wild social life and serious studying could not possibly mix. Others feel that a renaissance of spiritual interest was at hand.

This new interest in religion followed a decade of widespread use of "religion substitutes," the encounter groups and psychotherapies that did little to provide what the young adherents were looking for. The turn from humanistic philosophies—those that put man in the center of the universe—to theistic, or God-centered, religions seems to indicate that most people want and need to believe in a higher power than mere man.

It follows that if young people want to have a faith-centered relationship, they are likely to wait until they have gotten to know each other very well before they feel ready to commit to each other as they have committed to their belief in God. They are likely to see the random exercise of their sexuality as a form of immaturity rather than as a desirable life-style; their desire to protect each other from the consequences of possible pregnancy or disease will be stronger than any fleeting passion.

With less rebellion going on and the "generation gap" narrowing instead of widening, parents of college students may find their child's broadening education a stimulant to their own learning impulse. And, indeed, with their progeny at a critical point of life, it's a time for parents to reassess their own ambitions and unmet goals, which were postponed in the name of parenting.

One of the great pleasures of this period of parenting is that you are able to spend much more time alone with your spouse. Parenting activities are mostly confined to discussing situations and offering an opinion (whether that opinion is taken or not is another matter entirely), rather than feeding, bathing, and diapering. Parents also have the pleasure of being able to share their devotion with their child on a new basis, as peers, and hopefully as fellow worshippers.

The little child who once believed
That we were monarchs of the world
Is grown and sees us with new eyes
Even as we see him anew.
Please help us, Lord, let go of him
As You help him let go of us
So we may be, as strangers must,
Reborn as equals in Your love.

Regenerating

Adding a person to the family, whether by birth, adoption, or marriage, is always an ambivalent occasion. When the new addition is a daughter- or son-in-law, there are additional complications. Your child marries more than just another individual; their beloved comes equipped with a whole family, creating many new relationships with the attendant opportunities for caring and conflict.

Even the names for these new relatives—and for ourselves—may be strange at first and loaded with the extra significance that society bestows. Mother-in-law, for instance, is rarely associated with the loving Naomi, mother-in-law of the biblical Ruth, who out of caring urged her widowed daughter-in-law to marry again. More often, the association is with the mother-in-law character in crude jokes—a fool, a busybody, an overweight, disagreeable woman who wants her son back at all costs, even his happiness.

For some people, even the mention of an in-law brings back old unresolved resentment that originated at the time of their own marriage. But people are more than just their roles in the extended family would indicate, and it is best for all concerned—especially the new couple—to make the extra effort to find something to like about all the new relatives.

For some families, there is a long period of "getting to know you" before the wedding is announced; for others, there is scarcely enough time to shop for suitable clothing, much less adjust to the fact that your child will soon be a spouse. Either way, the relationship both parents have with their child must now reopen to include the intended.

The fact that the bride and groom come from different

families, perhaps widely divergent in culture and philosophy, makes the ceremonial aspects of the wedding very important. Many clergymen encourage couples to add meaningful readings to the standard prayers and vows, perhaps having some special way of acknowledging that for better or worse they are each bringing a family with them into the marriage.

Worshipping together as a new, extended family with your child's spouse's family promotes the kind of spiritual sharing you will want to be doing together when grandchildren are born. Being there for one another at this time, praying for the success of this new marital union, is a very concrete way of declaring before God that this marriage has everyone's blessing.

It's important to have faith in everyone's ability to adjust to one another. Sometimes, afraid of causing trouble, extended-family members refuse to tell one another what is bothering them. Instead of allowing themselves the human act of disagreeing, they bottle up all their hurts and annoyances. Under pressure, their bottles explode, of course, spewing forth words and actions they later regret.

Complaining isn't an effective way to deal with differences either, especially complaining to your child about your child-in-law. Placing your child between a spouse and a parent is a no-win situation: even if you win the battle, you lose the war. A better approach is to use the skills you developed as a parent when your child was very young. Being honest and straightforward, criticizing the behavior you dislike, but never the person, is more effective, because it clears the air. Unlike fights that escalate into full-scale combat situations, honest disagreements can lead to one of two things: a change in the disliked behavior by one contender or forgiveness and unconditional acceptance by the other. Either way, there is truce with growth. Remember, too, that like children, most people respond to your attitudes and unspoken feelings more than to your actual words. Trying to sound all sweetness and light while still feeling intense anger simply makes you seem phony—not polite.

A child's wedding can inspire even a long-married couple to see their own relationship through fresh eyes. This is especially true when it is the last child to be married off and the couple is now on their own again, with time and energy to refocus on themselves.

It's a time for recalling the parenting goals that were set so many years ago and a time for reformulating them into grandparenting goals, should you be granted that status. It's also a time for reassessing your marital goals and deciding whether and what changes you both want to make.

But most important, it's a time to remember what it was that attracted you to each other and how the lessons you have learned over your time together can be used to sweeten the years that remain.

> *As our house expands, Lord,*
> *Let it be with love;*
> *Please bless our new family*
> *As our child has been blessed with theirs.*
> *And in this time of change, Lord,*
> *Enlighten us to Your word:*
> *That we were kin long before we met;*
> *All children of Your glorious host.*

GRANDPARENTING

Becoming a grandparent is a whole new way of being part of the nurturing of a baby; it generally involves all of the pleasures but none of the drudgery. It's a special role, but one that has to have its boundaries defined by those who are affected by it: the grandparents, the grandchild, and the parents.

The first task of grandparenting is to learn how to take care of the parents so they can take care of their child. This starts in the parents' respective childhoods, so the grandparents-to-be can have input only into their own child, at least until the wedding. Then, their nurturing needs to be directed at the couple, encouraging them to be confident of their ability to raise a family, should they have one.

Just one note on that 'should they have one.' There is no 'decision to become a grandparent' and if there were one, it would not be yours. It is one area of life that you have absolutely no control over, nor do you want to meddle in if you don't want to damage your family and in-law relationships. In the time between the first edition of this book and today, the US birth rate has fallen dramatically, and the data put the average number of live births per woman at slightly under 1.75, which is far less than 'replacement' level, generally figured at 2.1 births per woman to factor in early deaths. So, if you think of this like a grandbaby lottery, you may feel like you've lost, rather than win at supporting the couple no matter what. So, while we're going to proceed on the assumption that becoming a grandparent is the natural next step, just a warning that just like becoming a parent, sometimes our best plans don't work out. So, don't ask, don't tell, don't beg. You can pray, and weigh in if you are asked, but this is the most intimate part of your child's life, and one you need to keep a matter-of-fact attitude about for the sake of their marriage.

During pregnancy, grandparents can help the young couple best by supporting their plans for the birth and care of the child. It is difficult to feel free to express feelings and ideas about child care when you feel you may be criticized by your own mother and mother-in-law for not doing things their way; it's even harder if you feel you may be hurting their feelings by expressing the intention to do the opposite of what they did. Some examples are planning to breast-feed when the grandmothers bottle-fed (or vice versa) or planning to deliver in the hospital when their children were born at home (or vice versa). Sometimes the best way to deal with these sensitive areas is to remember that childcare patterns tend to go in cycles, and what your children reject, your grandchildren will most likely embrace.

Grandparents-to-be are often tempted to buy tiny dresses or suits for their coming grandchild or else spend large amounts of money on nursery furniture and the like. Focusing instead on presents that help make the parents' adjustment easier—a heavy-duty washing machine, a freezer full of dinners, or housecleaning service for the first few months—frees them to give more of their attention to the baby.

Next to conflicts between the new mother and the new grandmother, the most disturbing clashes take place between the two new grandmothers. Sometimes the problem is based on jealousy, each one wanting to be the favorite grandmother, but occasionally it's an expression of deeper problems with the relationship between parent and grandparent, who still are, of course, parent and child.

The least effective solution is to take sides, because that only alienates everyone concerned. A better answer might be to seek an advisor who can mediate and help bring peace to the entire family; a pastoral counselor or member of the clergy can be a most effective family helper in this crisis.

Having a harmonious extended family is a blessing no child should be denied: even the new infant benefits from the warm feelings engendered at family ceremonies where there is that feeling of belonging. Although some people feel that exposing an infant to crowds may be dangerous, the advantages of being part of the family far outweigh the inconveniences, unless it is a particularly sickly child. It is helpful for the new parents to get out with others, too, especially their loved ones, who can be trusted to spend some time holding the baby. Many couples especially feel the desire to rejoin their religious community but fear that they might not be welcome with their little one. If the grandparents are available to accompany their children and grandchildren, there are enough adults to take turns entertaining the baby outside the sanctuary if things get a bit too loud.

Some grandparents love to baby-sit and are, in fact, insulted if they aren't asked; others would rather not change diapers and spoon-feed mashed bananas. Grandparents are as varied as their grandchildren: take nothing for granted. A good rule of thumb is to never assume your services as baby-sitting grandparents are wanted (until you're asked) and never feel obligated to comply. Since your children probably have firm ideas on childrearing, baby-sitting may come with a job description that you don't want to fill.

Although full-time or even occasional baby-sitting isn't necessarily part of being a grandparent, being a special person to your grandchild is. The nice thing about being a grandparent is that you have perspective. You don't get as nervous about your grandchild as you did about your child. You've learned through experience that babies survive an amazing number of bumps and scrapes. You can pass this confidence on to your grandchild in ways that his parents are as yet unable to.

You also have a more highly developed spiritual sense than you did when you were twenty or thirty years younger. You can see, and show your grandchild, the thousands of ways God shows Himself in everyday things—ways that your child may be too rushed and too tired to see.

When more grandchildren are born, you can give the older ones special time, away from brothers and sisters, with full adult attention. It's nice to be able to afford special toys and presents, but the best gift of all is the gift of yourself: to talk to, to bake cookies with, to learn the secrets of woodworking or photography or nature.

Many families have heirlooms that are handed down from generation to generation. Often a Bible, with records of births, marriages, and deaths, is part of the heritage. But technology presents new ways to create enduring memories of your family history, by recording interviews with older family members, reproducing old family photographs and letters, preserving the songs and celebrations, and beginning a collection of remembrances of your grandchildren's lives.

A record of one's ancestors, in any form, is especially helpful when talking to older children about marriage and families: it illustrates the persistence of the family as the most viable living arrangement.

The final task of grandparenting is simply to love your children's children, without reservation or conditions, to encourage them to love and obey their own parents, and to lead them into the light of the love of God. With love flowing through and around them, they cannot help but reflect its warmth on others and back upon themselves.

Lord, we ask Your blessing
For this tiny green bud
On our family tree:
This child of our child.
May the strength of our roots
Help him to flower
In the warmth of Your sun:
This soul of our soul.

Reversing

Middle age is a delightful time. Your children are on their own and, hopefully, have satisfying marriages that have begun to provide you with grandchildren to love. Your marriage has gone through the hard times and emerged stronger, your finances are probably more stable than they have ever been, and your personal style and spirituality have matured, more than compensating for the few facial lines and gray hairs your mirror might reveal. In short, your life is finally on an even keel.

But life is not lived in a vacuum; to some people it seems that they have barely begun to feel the freedom from the constant care of their children, when their aging parents start to need parenting.

This middle-aged crisis of role reversal—where all of a sudden the parents you leaned on for many years need to lean on you—can be frustrating. This is because, even though many of your parents' demands may seem adolescent (or younger) to you, your parents are still adults who need to control their own lives. The conflict comes when the adult children feel that their aged parents are trying to control their lives too.

The adult children first need to determine how much and what kind of help their parents need. Good nutrition and medical advances have increased the productive years most people have after retirement, although there may be illnesses and infirmities that narrow the parents' perspective on living. A gerontologist—a medical specialist in problems of the aged—may be especially helpful in sorting out which afflictions are part of the natural aging process and which are reversible.

It is especially important for an older person to have one primary physician to coordinate any special consultations or treatments that may become necessary. Since the elderly often have more than one problem, they are often given several medications. Some of these may be incompatible or may cause changes in behavior that may be misdiagnosed as psychiatric problems.

Some helplessness can actually be a sort of blackmail to get the adult children to pay more attention to the older parent. This may be a long-time way of relating or may just be a natural outgrowth of the loneliness that accompanies the loss of old friends and neighbors. The healthiest way to treat this kind of inappropriate dependency is to get your parents involved in new activities with other older people. Many churches and community centers sponsor senior-citizen day programs, complete with lunch and assistance with issues such as financial and housing problems. These can provide an atmosphere conducive to making new friends to replace the ones who have died or moved away.

At some point, most couples have to face the decision of whether to bring a parent (or parents) to live with them or to find a nursing home or intermediate care facility. Sometimes the question arises because the parents have grown too fragile to continue to run their own home; other situations include the terminally ill parent and the one who has severe psychiatric disability or other medical problem. In any case, the decision should be a mutual one, made by the elderly person and their entire family.

Years ago, care of the aging parents usually fell to the eldest daughter. Now, with health insurance and alternative care situations readily available, plus eldest daughters (and the other children) returning to or remaining in the work force during the years their parents need additional care, the issue is not so clearcut. Since there are so many different choices (and combinations of choices), the easiest way to decide what is best for the particular family is to consider the needs of the parents and how they can best be met without conflicting severely with the needs of their children.

The first area to consider is physical care. It's easy to assume, if one or both parents need quite a bit of help with bathing, feeding, and so forth, that this can best be accomplished by a nursing home. Other alternatives include family care, a paid home health aide (sometimes covered by insurance), and some combination of the two. Your local office on aging can provide information on resources. Some communities have hospice-care visiting nurses and assistants for the terminally ill person who wishes to remain with the family rather than enter a hospital or nursing home.

The second area is the emotional one. Moving in with their children can be a source of both pleasure and pain for elderly parents. Although they may enjoy seeing their grandchildren growing up, the loss of their own friends and neighbors may be overwhelming. If they have lived in the same house for all their married life, attending the same church and shopping at the same stores, they may find the changes involved in the move disorienting and stressful. For some adults who need help with medications but are otherwise capable of self-care, a senior citizen hotel may be a viable alternative; note well, though, that these establishments vary greatly in quality. The loss of privacy may not be too high a price to pay to be in the company of other older adults who can provide satisfying companionship. Some gerontologists even feel that the social life helps prevent the emotional and spiritual depressions that some elderly people are prone to.

Safety is an important concern, too, when evaluating housing for older adults. Often overlooked are household furniture and appliances that turn into hazards with the decrease in agility and vision that usually accompanies aging. Bathtubs may suddenly become impossible to get into without assistance, and a brief dizzy spell may bring disaster if it happens on top of a stepladder.

Most senior citizen homes have special safety features—grab bars in the bathroom, low-pile wall-to-wall carpeting, hand rails in halls—that can easily be duplicated in any home. Other safety issues tend to really be matters of judgment, such as not smoking in bed, being careful with the stove, and so on. If judgment has declined severely because of dementia or other degenerative disease, a constant companion may be essential regardless of where the person actually lives.

Finally, there is the matter of spiritual needs. These are really twofold: the kind that is satisfied by going to church and the kind that requires inward peace and outward solitude. Going to church also meets many of an older person's social needs and keeps their perspective open to others' cares and requirements, as well as their own spiritual needs. But the need to make peace with yourself and God is a private matter requiring private space.

Unfortunately, space considerations often make it impossible for the older adult living with family to be the sole occupant of a bedroom. Financial considerations create the necessity for housing nursing home inhabitants living two or more to a room. This also ignores the need for some truly private time, not unlike what often happens to children. It is doubly important that an older person feel some measure of control over their life, which is difficult if they feel they've been forced into a dormitory life-style.

Yet often the family must do the best they can with the available resources. This is why the decision needs to be made by the entire family. If the aging parents have several sons and daughters but only one or two take the responsibility for their care, jealousy, anger, and guilt can divide the family. The child whose home the parent moves into (or who lives the closest to the nursing home) can end up being torn by conflicting responsibilities to parents, children, spouse, siblings, and job. If the parent is very ill or requires constant supervision, the primary caretaker can feel very tied down, almost like having a newborn but without the pleasures and knowledge that the constant neediness will soon be outgrown.

Overwhelming health needs may mean the nursing home issue has to be reconsidered after the parent moves in with a child. The solution is never final, so a periodic family conference may be in order with the siblings other than the primary caretaker being assigned specific duties to give some respite to the host family.

As life draws to a close, elderly people often seem to withdraw into themselves, emerging less and less frequently. When they do emerge, it may be to share some thoughts about their past. This "life review," as gerontologists call it, gives the older person a way of measuring the worth of their life.

Listening to your parent's life review may also deepen your insight and help you reinterpret the painful moments in your past relationship with this parent. The lesson the elderly teach is that it is never too late to acknowledge our human shortcomings, forgive one another, and learn to love more deeply and without conditions.

The death of one parent is often devastating to the remaining one. There may be mixed feelings, especially if the death was preceded by a long illness or profound loss of function, on the part of the surviving spouse and children. If they can be open with each other, remembering the good times and bad, giving each other solace but always acknowledging that the departed one was a human being, not a saint, the family can begin to mourn their loss together. To grow closer rather than become isolated from each other can be a good outcome of bereavement.

For some, however, the overwhelming response to the death of a parent is guilt, which usually comes from some unfinished business between the bereaved and the deceased, perhaps a longstanding disagreement, or just not having enough time to say good-bye.

Making peace with your parents can be a simple matter of telling them that you love them; it really is no different from making peace with your adult children.

Although it is the parents' role to set limits on their children's behavior when they are very young, and perhaps it becomes their role to set behavioral limits on their own parents in their twilight years, it is never appropriate to set limits on love.

God's love for His children is unconditional and unlimited: it is our own greatest pleasure and glory to reflect that love on our children and our parents.

Give us time, Lord,
Time enough to see
The purpose You give
To our humble lives;
And if our time on earth
Is to be brief, O Lord,
Let us not waste a moment
In hatred and blame.

Reflecting

I used to think that if the angels graced our humble home, they would come at night. With two active teenagers filling all available space with bicycles and schoolbooks and with snacks hastily—and not always thoroughly—cleared from the kitchen table; with the shouts and laughter of friendship and the squabbles and tears of siblinghood; and with us, two happily married adults, slipping and falling headlong into the pitfalls of day-to-day existence, forgetting as often as not to think before we speak, even the most perfect angel would have a hard time finding a place to perch, much less a moment of peace to think angelic thoughts. How much more hospitable the cool, silent house was in the predawn hours, that lull before the storm in which I spent my solitary moments putting these ideas and dreams on paper in 1985.

Now, 34 years later, having seen those teenagers turn into responsible adults and having seen my partner in parenting through a long illness with inevitable decline to death four years ago, I recall that time with fondness. And, as I sit back, having just finished working through the original manuscript, making nips and tucks, updates and typo fixes, I seem to have not moved much from that peaceful place, where life goes on, yet the theme song seems to remain: Lennon and McCartney, *In My Life*, a remnant of my youth.

But back to those angels, whose visitation I questioned at the end of the first edition.

I have learned—been taught—while writing and rewriting this book, that I was presumptuous to have thought so. The angels are here now: in the midst of all our noise and confusion, their glory and mercy—the grace of parenting—gently enters our souls, our hearts, our stubborn minds. They are here, even though we do our best to ignore them, intent as we are on the "realities of life."

They are here because we are parents; because parenthood being both receptive and reflective, is an act of grace; because we seek to inspire those children whose very presence has inspired us. They are here to remind us of our reason for being.

We have chosen this vocation;
We have been chosen for this vocation.
It is evidence of our will;
It is evidence of our Creator's will.
Our children are bound to us
Even as we are bound to our Creator,
By a fragile, pulsing cord
Dissolving at one end,
Growing stronger at the other.

ABOUT THE AUTHOR

There are "official" bios of me on various business sites, all to be taken with a grain of salt, please. The important things have little or nothing to do with what is there.

These are my proudest achievements:

Long, long ago, I was a La Leche League Leader in New York City for ten years, during which time I served as president of the city's chapter, helped many mothers, grew many new leaders, lost my fear of public speaking, and made many lifelong friends. With babies on our laps, often nursing (discreetly) wherever we were, trying to make the world safer for mothering, we shared our joys and sorrows. (If you are reading this and we've lost touch, please find me!) I also served on the advisory boards of many organizations devoted to the rights of families, too many to remember details of. My main qualification for this was the desire to change the world for my babies, now two delightful adults. I also learned how to get people to work together, even though no salary was involved. This would prove useful when I became an entrepreneur.

I've been a consultant, managed two human resource departments, was president of a family-owned sheet metal manufacturing company, served as adjunct faculty and dissertation consultant for several institutions and as forensic consultant and expert witness in cases involving civil rights, sexual harassment, wrongful termination, ethical professional practice, and related matters, was a volunteer homebirth midwife, and family therapist, not exactly in that order. And through it all, it was family first, both for me and for those in my employ.

Now, it's entrepreneur that most easily describes me. I wrote my first line of code in high school and developed the architecture for a new technology, which you can learn more about on my website, should this interest you. What drove me was twofold. One, my desire to never have someone else make me retire, and two, my desire to make it easier for people to have great personal relationships. And I did it, even though it the world of technology, being female is regarded as only slightly stranger than having two heads. And, with tip of hat to the late great Frank Sinatra, I did it my way.

That way always put the inspiration of parenting, the essence of concern for the future, at the forefront of my life. And that is why I smile so much.

Find Janice at: http://www.teamingscience.com

Curious about other Crossroad Press books?
Stop by our site:
http://store.crossroadpress.com
We offer quality writing
in digital, audio, and print formats.